THE MYTH
OF ATLAS

Families and the
Therapeutic Story

By

Maurizio Andolfi, M.D.
Claudio Angelo, M.D.

and

Marcella de Nichilo, Ph.D.

Family Therapy Institute of Rome

Edited and Translated by
Vincenzo F. DiNicola, M.D.
University of Ottawa, Ontario, Canada

Brunner/Mazel *Publishers* • New York

Library of Congress Cataloging-in-Publication Data

Andolfi, Maurizio.
    [Tempo e mito nella psicoterapia familiare. English]
    The myth of Atlas : families and the therapeutic story / by
Maurizio Andolfi, Claudio Angelo, and Marcella de Nichilo ;
edited and translated by Vincenzo F. DiNicola.
      p. cm.
    Translation of: Tempo e mito nella psicoterapia familiare.
    Bibliography: p.
    Includes indexes.
    ISBN 0-87630-549-4
    1. Family psychotherapy.   I. Angelo, Claudio.   II. de Nichilo, Marcella.
III. DiNicola, Vincenzo F.   IV. Title.
RC488.5.A4913 1989
616.89′156—dc20   89–32190
                                                        CIP

Originally published as *Tempo e Mito Nella Psicoterapia Familiare*
Copyright © 1987 by Editore Boringhieri SpA, Torino

Copyright © 1989 by Brunner/Mazel, Inc.

Published by
BRUNNER/MAZEL, INC.
19 Union Square
New York, New York 10003

MANUFACTURED IN THE UNITED STATES OF AMERICA

10 9 8 7 6 5 4 3 2 1

Foreword

Authors do not hold sole title to their works—or so literary critics claim. Readers, they say, also have rights of authorship. They may bring their own framings, using their life experience to give new dimensions to the work. They have the right to introduce nuance and chiaroscuro where the author drew clear definitions.

As a reader of Sophocles, Freud shaped the Oedipus tale, turning a specific Greek myth into a metaphor for universal family dynamics. Now Andolfi and his coauthors, following again from the Greek, rewrite the Atlas myth as a metaphor for the piling of all family members' burdens on the shoulders of one—Dino, the identified patient of the Penna family. But unlike Freud's retelling, this Atlas myth fits only the Pennas, involving Dino, his mother, and his seven siblings as coauthors in the writing of the new script.

At first glance this seems a useful formula for resolving the complex problem of the therapeutic encounter. As constructivists, family therapists have always held that coauthoring the family narrative, moving it from the rigidity of a single reading to the promising complexity of multiple perspectives, is the therapeutic route *par excellence*.

But here's the rub. This schema leaves the therapist at the beginning of the road. How do you select from the Joycean grammar of family interactions the bits that will be significant for the construction of a therapeutic alternative? How do you encourage coauthorship by family members? How do you promote acceptance of the new myth as a better edition of the previous one? And last but not least, why does it matter? None of these questions are answered by the constructivist framework per se.

Andolfi and his colleagues have invited us readers to join them in their trek of exploration in healing, and they have made the roadmap of their search admirably accessible. First they give a view of the family, then of the therapist and the therapeutic process, and last the ingredients necessary for myth-making. Let me trace the complexity and simplicity of their trip.

In Whitaker's metaphor, families send their delegates to reproduce themselves psychologically. The authors explore this premise, combining Kelly's concept of individual constructs with clinical notions of family therapists working with three-generational families. The family story as carried by the family members is maintained by relational metaphors, roles, functions, and rituals. It is, therefore, resistant to change, but it evolves through time and crisis.

Therapy is seen as a process of joining and challenging. The provocation of the authors' earlier work has been softened and clarified, but it is still very much a central ingredient of therapy: provocation with support, provocation with respect, provocation of the system and support for the individual, and so on. The therapist is a connector of two with a third, a constructor of triangles. The third side may be another family member, the therapist, a concrete object, or a metaphor. Throughout this process, context, hierarchies, proximity and distance, affect, cognition, reading of meanings, and behaviors are constantly shifting.

In the therapist's interventions, s/he is playful and provocative, concrete and mysterious, discontinuous, involved and distant. S/he is always keeping at least six red balls of meaning in the air, and each one provides different positions for the symptom bearer and the family members.

Myth-making is as always a dialectic process. Family members offer behaviors. The therapist attaches meaning. If the initial probe is sufficiently ambiguous, a family member may provide a useful modification. If the therapist is alert, and lucky, s/he will expand that. And so the process continues, each offering words to the other until the words become familiar and carry shared meaning. While the therapist and family member engage in myth-making, behaviors are given new meaning and come to be seen as consistent with the new/old script.

I hope Andolfi, Angelo, and de Nichilo will agree with my reading of their work. But the work is there, ready to be enriched by your own association. The trek is not easy, but it is always exciting. The authors may challenge some of your cherished beliefs, but they do offer others. You are the prism.

Salvador Minuchin, M.D.
New York, New York

To Carl Whitaker, an exemplary teacher
To our families of origin
To Lotte, Paolo, Marzia, Philipp, and to Diego

Contents

Preface

This book comes ten years after the American publication of my first book, *Family Therapy: An Interactional Approach* (1979) and follows six years after another, *Behind the Family Mask* (1983), in collaboration with Angelo, Menghi, and Nicolò-Corigliano. My first interesting reflection is to discover elements of continuity, along with those of change from the past, running through the various steps of this journey. A constant element inspiring all three books is a deep-rooted conviction that the family, as a complex and dynamic system in evolution, possesses the resources necessary to assure both belonging and progressive autonomy to its members.

Starting from these premises, the therapist can solicit, rediscover, activate, and channel these resources, but he certainly cannot introduce them *de novo* from the outside or search for them elsewhere if they are missing from the family. From this point of view, the emergence of pathology is seen as a critical moment in the evolution of a family that seems incapable of using its own resources at a particular stage of its development. After some time, this incapacity can make excessive and disorderly demands on these resources, or it can produce an actual developmental "block." Seeing mental illness in a developmental framework is the aspect of our work that has most stimulated the growth of our ideas in the past few years.

Another constant that has guided our clinical work and teaching and can be found on different levels in these three books is the position of the therapist in the construction of the therapeutic story. The therapist is called upon to use himself fully by entering the family story and by taking the same risks that he expects of the family. For example, if he wants the family to move and overcome its own resistance in order to regain greater authenticity, he cannot stay still and watch without revealing himself personally.

We have often asked ourselves if there is more pathology in the actions of our clients or in our heads, when we are unable to understand their experience in developmental terms. The therapeutic struggle itself seems to consist of learning how to "normalize" the hypotheses that we formulate in therapy and, more generally, in our way of thinking. Experience has convinced us that when we succeed in doing this, the family accepts us as "insiders" and moves toward change with less difficulty and in less time. This challenge of always looking for the positive in families without getting caught up in labels of pathology is something I learned from my teacher, Sal Minuchin, whose influence has become a pillar of my clinical work.

My first book, *Family Therapy: An Interactional Approach*, is the most technical one, aimed at outlining interventions and providing a therapeutic structure, following the family's change step by step. In that book, the therapist moves within a kind of "theory of technique" prevalent in the 1970s and based on the strategic intervention and resolution of symptoms.

Behind the Family Mask represents our first attempt to shift to a higher level. From the analysis of the family's rules and of the strategies in the session, we began to search for and to experiment with a complex therapeutic relationship that permits us to "support the individual while provoking the system." Therapeutic provocation in rigid systems has become a model for the Institute of Family Therapy in Rome, where for many years we have been involved with families with a psychotic member, in order to respond to the pressing demands for psychotherapy with these families, following the deinstitutionalization that began in Italy in 1978.

In *Behind the Family Mask* the therapist is again presented as the hero of the therapeutic struggle, in spite of our greater effort to elaborate a theory, especially about the definition of the therapeutic system. The distinction between "family at risk" and "family designated rigid" was a first attempt to re-evaluate the developmental phases of the family and to consider the designation of illness as a response to change. That book concludes by posing an important question: how to consider the individual in a systemic perspective.

The individual and his process of development within the family, in both normal phases and pathological ones, became a stimulating problem, posing many questions for the authors of *Behind the Family Mask* and for the development of the Rome Institute in general. Important debates over the complex relationship between the family and the individual began within the Institute of Family Therapy, whose first findings were published in a special issue of our journal, *Terapia Familiare*, demonstrating the need for further investigations of this theme which involve both individual and family therapists.

The method of observing the individual and how to consider him in relation to the family brings us to the first differentiation among the authors of *Behind the Family Mask*. Each of us started to explore the avenue which is most congenial to his or her own intellectual curiosity and therapeutic sensibility. One of the authors followed the avenue into group work, another into Kleinian psychotherapy, and the authors of this current book took a developmental path that frames the individual in a trigenerational dimension.

This book is the result of clinical reflections that add another dimension to our previous formulations of family therapy. Moving from a model of the nuclear family to include the generation of the grandparents in our conceptual schema has not only allowed us to add more people to the session, but has also been a way to better understand the individual. Through specific ways of interacting with the trigenerational family, the individual appears as a complex entity, full of contradictions and conflicts. For the observer, however, they become tools for understanding the individual's internal world when trying to grasp the implicit links between current behaviors and experiences and the unmet needs of the past. Above all, Carl Whitaker, to whom this book is dedicated, has inspired me through our encounters over the years to grow as a therapist and expand my concept of the family in therapy.

The study of myths has been extremely useful in our attempt to grasp the historical, developmental aspect of the family. We asked ourselves if the degree to which each person can change over time is closely dependent on the degree of freedom that he is allowed by the family myth and, consequently, by the greater or lesser rigidity of the role and functions that he fulfils at home.

We consider myths as mobile structures that are constructed and modified over time. Through their elaboration in therapy we help the individual members of the family distance themselves from what is represented in myth in prescriptive terms, but at the same time to accept the parts of the myth that do not conflict with their search for a personal identity.

We have used time as a fundamental parameter to evaluate change in the developmental progression of the family, especially when it has created a block for itself. And in the end, we used it to scan the phases of therapy, in an alternation of joining and separation between therapist and family.

Among other things, in this book we have again taken up and expanded the concept of provocation in therapy, emphasizing the fact that to be therapeutic, provocation must always be accompanied by a joining attitude. That is, it must succeed in communicating that the therapist "is standing by the system while he is provoking it."

In another chapter we have expanded a theme that is dear to me, the use of play in therapy, not only to outline its usefulness as a technique (see *Family Therapy: An Interactional Approach*), but especially to emphasize the need for the *therapist to learn how to play*. If he is able to rediscover the value of play in itself, he will learn not to take himself too seriously and to consider his own and others' constructions of reality as temporary and changeable, in order to introduce flexibility and uncertainty into his own cognitive operations.

If *Behind the Family Mask* is the product of a group at work and represented an important period of fervor for the Institute of Family Therapy in Rome, this book—representing a more reflective and committed phase of our work—is the result of an intense collaboration between Claudio Angelo, Marcella de Nichilo, and myself. The credit for the realization of this book goes above all to Claudio. Without the dedication and cast-iron discipline that brought him by train to Rome from Bolzano in the Alps every two weeks during the last four years, I would not have been able to stop to discuss every single point in the book and define with him the guidelines to reflect on and write about during the intervals. Marcella inspired our work with her ideas and comments and participated with us in this book by writing the final chapter on the myth of Atlas. The therapeutic process described in her chapter involving the Penna family is an integral contribution to the book, and it coherently punctuates and synthesizes the contents of the preceding chapters. We took it as our title as it captured the spirit of the book.

Writing this book has been a shared enterprise in which the quality of our exchanges and personal motivations were the basis for the construction of this book. Examples taken from our clinical cases became tied up with the stories and myths of our own families that, here and there, also appear in the book, incognito.

Even the organization of our work was influenced by our very different and complementary styles. I, who can only write with a pen, have kept up the tradition—writing, rewriting, and crumpling up dozens of sheets of paper at my desk. Claudio, fascinated by the latest computer models, has introduced the "new myths" of technology to give us clean and clear drafts of our manuscript. Marcella, who is also a scholar in languages and literature, contributed to the reshaping of the American edition of this book.

My recurrent working trips abroad, in Europe and in North and South America, have allowed me to think over and to explain some of the ideas that we were developing in Rome, working them out in consultations with more varied families from many different geographic and social contexts. All of this has enriched me with transcultural comments and reflections that I have brought back to our "think tank" in Rome, and has convinced me that the universality of suffering and the capacity for renewal in every family transcend the specifics of particular cultures.

June 1989   *Maurizio Andolfi*
                                                                        Rome

Acknowledgments

First, we want to thank our families in treatment and our students in training, both of whom have given us the permission to train and to explore in real life what we were elaborating theoretically in our book.

Next, we wish to thank our colleagues who are teachers at the Rome Institute of Family Therapy: Katia Giacometti, who gave our manuscript a careful and critical reading and provided us with her valuable suggestions, as she has done for many years; Anna Nicolò, for her useful and precise advice on numerous aspects of the book; Carmine Saccu, for a number of creative notions about children in therapy; and Silvia Soccorsi, to whom we are indebted for numerous ideas about the themes of joining and separation.

Bobbie Cassin, who is a dear friend, deserves our thanks for having followed our work over the years. She translated some of our previous publications, read some parts of this book, and recommended Dr. DiNicola as our translator.

We wish to express our special gratitude to Vincenzo F. DiNicola, M.D., who has been much more than a translator for the American edition of this book. First, he has integrated into his work some of our theoretical ideas and clinical methods by having studied with us in Rome; and now he has enriched our book by providing his editorial comments and by provoking us with his transcultural feedback. Since we worked closely together on the American edition, we have incorporated all comments and clarifications for the English reader into the body of the text and in footnotes.

Last, we deeply regret the tragic loss of Ann Alhadeff, our editor at Brunner/Mazel. Ann was intimately involved in the process of editing this book in English, through extensive consultations with us and with the translator. We wish to acknowledge our debt to her fine editorial work and extend our deepest sympathy to her family and to her associates at Brunner/Mazel.

CHAPTER 1

The Construction of the Therapeutic Story

THE THERAPIST AS A RELATIONAL LINK

Our experiences with therapy over the past five years and the changes of theory that developed from them, along with the inevitable therapeutic modifications, have led us to reconsider what we espoused in our previous publications (Andolfi & Angelo, 1981; Andolfi et al., 1983). In our previous work, we demonstrated, among other things, how the family's therapeutic dilemma is characterized by its incapacity to tolerate the disorganization necessary to modify its homeostasis at one stage of development in order to acquire a new one that is more suitable to the next stage. We emphasized how this is expressed in the family's demand to "help it move, while allowing it to stand still" (Andolfi et al., 1983, p. 7). In this contradictory situation, the family tries to make the therapist play parts and roles that are most congruent with the maintenance of the status quo. We considered this strategy as *resistance to change* and it was strongly discouraged, if not directly opposed, as being unproductive. In reality, at a more subjective level, this resistance was perceived by the therapist as a rejection of his interventions and of therapy. This feeling of rejection and futility often pushed the therapist to attempt

1

to upset, right from the beginning, the family's self-image, by actively opposing the family's attempts to involve him[1] in a play or story apparently without a goal.

What we ignored, however, was that in the very act of opposing their story, the therapist's participation and involvement were already implicit, making him part of the family story.[2] If in practice this made it impossible to maintain an external position as a neutral observer, it would have been more useful first to *support* the family story and then, from within this new configuration of relationships, *to construct a therapeutic story.* We are now less interested in theoretical formulations and strategies of paradoxical interventions (Haley, 1977; Selvini Palazzoli et al., 1978a; Watzlawick, Weakland, & Fisch, 1974; Weeks & L'Abate, 1982), which reduce the field of observation. In particular, we refrained from formulating hypotheses about family functioning which exclude the therapist as an interacting subject and fail to focus on the therapeutic context as the proper place for elaborating and verifying these hypotheses. It was exactly this attention to the subject, to the individual therapist's cognitive and emotional states, that moved us away from concepts that were rigidly supra-individual[3] and led us to study the therapeutic context as a meeting place and for forming new choices and experiences as described by others (Ackerman, 1966; Bowen, 1978; Minuchin, 1974; Napier & Whitaker, 1978; Rotondo, 1983;

---

[1]About gender pronouns: For the sake of brevity, when "we" appears in this book, the reference is to the work of the authors. For the sake of brevity, the therapist is referred to by the masculine gender pronoun. The clumsy "he or she" is used only when it is necessary to refer to both members of a conjugal pair, for example. Interestingly, this is not problematic in Italian, where gender pronouns are neutral.—Translator

[2]In Italian "storia" has several layers of meaning, including here both "story" as narrative and "history" as chronology. In this book, the word "story" should be read with both meanings.—Translator

[3]"This concept brings together and defines the position of those who choose the family as a system of interactions as their object of analysis and intervention, abandoning any attempt to conceptualize the individual in terms that do not see them as members of a system" (Giacometti, 1979, p. 14).

Satir, 1967, 1972). In this dimension, either the acceptance or the rejection by the therapist of attributions that the family makes about him become part of the construction of a new system—the therapeutic system—leaving aside whatever intentions the family has in making its attributions.

This does not mean that the actions of the therapist make no difference, but only that he cannot predict what effect they will have on the family, except in a very general way. On the other hand, he cannot predict what effect the family's interventions will have on him. The only consequence that he can reasonably predict is that every attempt to change the values[4] and the rules that maintain the balance of the system produces a certain degree of movement in the opposite direction, to counteract any sudden imbalances. It is, then, useful to shift our attention to the fact that what is therapeutic about his interventions seems to be more attributable to the therapist's capacity to remain consistent in his own attitudes and behavior and in the meanings that he is offering to the family. In other words, the therapist's effectiveness depends on his capacity to maintain his integrity and to draw personal boundaries clearly enough to serve as models for the individual members of the system (see Minuchin's, 1974, notion of *modeling*) during the process of individuation and the consequent changes in the rules of interaction.

If, on the one hand, the therapist is required to have his own internal integrity or coherence—an "I position" as Bowen (Anonymous, 1972) calls it—on the other hand, it is necessary that the therapist "set up a useful atmosphere of rapport, a touching quality of contact" (Ackerman, 1966, p. 268). In 1966, Ackerman was already stressing the need to "move directly into the stream of family conflict, to energize and influence the interactional processes" (Ackerman, 1966, p. 268). But at the same time he described the need to know how to separate oneself and acquire an observing ego: "He

---

[4]By "values" we mean here the sum of cognitive and emotional attributions of meaning the family makes about the world it lives in.

withdraws to objectify his experience, to survey and assess significant events and move back in again" (Ackerman, 1966, p. 268). This moving in and out, this "weighing and balancing the sick and helpful emotional forces" requires "a flexible, open and undefensive use of the self" by the therapist (Ackerman, 1966, p. 268). The value that the therapist's self comes to acquire in his rapport with the family, together with the fact that most of his interventions are made through the identified patient or other family members *in a personal relationship*, pose these problems: (a) What is the therapist's position in the therapeutic process? (b) What is the structure of the therapeutic relationship? (c) How should the individual member be considered in the family system?

In previous publications (Andolfi & Angelo, 1981), we described how the family can make the therapist play predetermined roles in the session during the reediting of the "family drama" in order to maintain its acquired equilibrium. As the family reenacts this drama in the session, the members make demands of the therapist originally directed to another member of the system. The therapist can become the temporary target of all their projections. In this way, for example, the family "script" can call for a more loving father or a more mature partner ("more" refers, usually implicitly, to the real father or partner). The therapist can be solicited to take on one of these functions precisely because there do not seem to be other "actors" capable of doing it within the family. To avoid playing this assigned part seems of little therapeutic use, as does playing it without being aware of it. If, instead, the therapist accepts the invitation, takes the part, and interprets it, he can "feel in his own skin" what each of the family members expects from a loving father or a mature partner. By temporarily filling important gaps or voids, the therapist can gather vital information about the meaning of those gaps for the various family members. What is really missing and what is ideally hoped for can then become part of the therapeutic story.

When even more magical functions come to be requested of the therapist—perhaps to be godlike—it may be more useful to accept this investiture than to refuse to play along. If the therapist can use himself as the image of a god long enough to become a *relational metaphor*, he may be able to grasp the different needs of a Superior Being for different members. Then, the need for such an extraordinary being can be related to the absence of a reassuring parent for one or of marital support for another. In this way, developing and amplifying the meanings attached to the search for a divinity, differences and complementarities can be pointed out between the needs of A and B, allowing each one, including the therapist, to perform the triangulation necessary to orient oneself to the specific problem.

In this conception of therapy, the therapist continually positions himself on one of the sides of various triangles. This is as true when the therapist poses as external activator and observer of interactive processes, as in the moments when he acts as a mirror or model for the others in the course of their interactions. This is not less "systemic" for the therapist to continually enter into an individual rapport with each of the members of a family in the process of gathering information from them. According to many family theorists and clinicians, among them Selvini Palazzoli and associates (1980a), this procedure demands instead a position of neutrality on the part of the therapist. *It is not necessary for the therapist to give up using himself (as a whole thinking and feeling being) as the principal link for gathering information, in order to maintain himself constantly at a metalevel with respect to the family system.*

If information consists of the identification of differences, and difference implies a relationship (Bateson, 1979), it seems inevitable that the first component of differentiation is the therapist himself at the moment he adds himself as a third person in a dyadic relationship. One of the structural elements of therapy resides precisely in the therapist's possibility of occupying alternate positions. He can observe and stabilize the dyadic bond now with one, then with the other participant, placing himself as a third observer of what is unfolding. We are referring here to the triangular structure, which is the only one to permit each person to "enter and leave the relationship," to distance oneself long enough to understand what is happening, and to create for oneself models from which to learn. Just as the therapist learns (when he poses as observer) the rules and the relational styles of the different dyads which he activates, so does each partner (who assists in the interactions between the therapist and the other member of the dyad) learn new ways of interacting, modeled in part on what he or she sees done by the therapist when he responds to given functional demands.

The therapist can be, in turn, caring or detached, supportive or provocative. He knows how to use the expectations of others to enter into a relationship with each of them and how to break it off. He is a model and a reference point for them. Entering as a third side of different triangles and activating from the outside new triadic dimensions, the therapist constructs a therapeutic story. In so doing, the therapist models a complete relationship, which accentuates elements of diversification and specificity, rather than reducing the world to terms the family already takes for granted. This approach transforms the collection of information based on observed and predictable facts into a search for new links between individuals and their personal views of the world.

Continually creating new triangular relationships and trying to tie together different triangles becomes one of the principal tasks of the therapist when he poses as activator of different relationships. For us, the key way to enter into a relationship with the family and to introduce a method of working in the session is by discerning patterns, selecting those that seem most significant, and proposing new ones by amplifying the old, familiar ones. The more the therapist succeeds in binding and unbinding, structuring and restructuring the bonds, the more each of them, including the therapist, will be able to try out new relational positions and therefore learn new ways of being and of acting in relation to others.

In order to propose himself as the relational link[5] for the family, the therapist must also be equal to the task of grasping the "world" of each member, that is, of identifying with some of his or her very specific and personal aspects. He must discover the circumstances in which each member is inclined to involve himself and to take direct risks to change the family. It becomes indispensable for the therapist to use his eyes and ears in order to understand quickly how each one imagines the first encounter and the successive ones, what potential alternative scenarios he is inclined to fantasize about, what risks and what challenges are tolerable and at what times, without interrupting the flow of the relationship.

THE FIRST TELEPHONE CALL

The first moment of this process is represented by the first telephone call a member of the family makes to contact the therapist. At this time, the problem is presented to an expert who is asked to provide a solution. However, the context in which the dialogue takes place, influenced by the telephone, poses particular limits on the time, the contents, and the purpose of the conversation compared to a face-to-face session (see DiBlasio, Fischer, & Prata, 1986; Selvini Palazzoli et al., 1980a).

The time given to the person who telephones to make an appointment is limited in comparison to what he has "permission" to give in other circumstances. The need to explain

---

[5]By this term we do not mean a specific therapeutic technique, but an attitude (entering into contact with specific and emotionally relevant aspects of the "world" of the interlocutor) similar to that indicated by the term "joining" (Minuchin, 1974; Minuchin & Fishman, 1981). Joining has been misinterpreted to the point that it has almost come to mean putting people at ease—acting pleasantly or using the clichéd expressions of courtesy which a well-meaning host displays toward his guests.

the problem in general terms often offers the caller a chance to introduce arguments and to take a role that might be denied to him in the session. The therapist's attitude is decisive in this regard, in the sense that he, by evaluating the opportunity to give more or less time to what the speaker is saying about specific aspects of the relationship, agrees to prolong or to limit the conversation. Regardless of how things really are, whoever calls finds it necessary to anticipate in part which things the therapist will want to know more fully and which things will help the caller to establish a good relationship with him.

Whether the caller is the one who feels most involved in the problem, or the one who was delegated to present the problem, he takes on the function of intermediary for the family and guarantor of its equilibrium in his encounter with the therapist, to whom he brings a *proposal of a relationship*. At the same time, on a personal level, the caller finds himself in a position with the therapist to attempt an alliance or disengagement that permits him to acquire a position of advantage in family relations or to help to improve them or, on the other hand, to maintain the established balance and advantages.

The therapist, for his part, finds himself faced with the task of meeting the caller's request and of exploring any possible meanings or of refuting them. He begins to "construct" triangular hypotheses and to translate them into questions that try to amplify the elements revealed by the caller and to introduce suggestions for new links. To do this, he must succeed in establishing a bond with the most meaningful aspects of the family's relationships. He must reach those aspects with the greatest emotional content which will solicit a desire for a therapeutic rapport, after having touched a nerve.

We have an example in the following dialogue, which takes place between the therapist and a mother who asked for help for her 19-year-old daughter, Vittoria, who has confined herself to her own home, giving up her work and all contact with the outside world.

Therapist: But did she confine herself to home or to her own room?

Mother: She stays home and most of the time she's locked up in her own room . . .

Therapist: So she has a room of her own?

Mother: Yes, she has her own room.

Therapist: And who are in the other rooms?

Mother: In the other rooms? Well, there's her sister . . .

Therapist: And how old is her sister?

Mother: Her sister is 12.

Therapist: And does your 12-year-old go more willingly to the room of the 19-year-old or vice-versa?

Mother: Well, even the 12-year-old, after seeing her so irritable, has backed off . . . since my daughter doesn't want to be disturbed . . . not that she goes in anymore.

Therapist: And who else is at home?

Mother: Then there's my husband . . .

Therapist: And do you share the same room?

Mother: Of course!

Therapist: So you have three bedrooms. . . . Do any other people live with you?

Mother: No. We've always lived on our own.

Therapist: Would all the people who live in these rooms be willing to come here?

Mother: Well, you know, as far as my younger daughter is concerned, and maybe even the older one, I might manage to bring them along, since the older one doesn't want to hear about psychologists. But my husband is very busy and I don't know if he'll manage to find the time . . .

Therapist: So you have more trouble with your husband than with your daughter . . .

Mother: Well, yeah, for these things he's not very dependable.

Therapist: Ah-ha! . . . And why then do you have more need
of therapy for your daughter, if you tell me you've got
these problems with your husband?

Mother: (seems annoyed) But now my problem is my daughter
who doesn't go out. My husband lives his own life, he
comes and goes and does his thing as usual . . .

Therapist: So your daughter spends too much time at home
and your husband spends too much time outside . . .

Mother: You could put it that way . . . actually my husband
always tends to delegate the solutions to these problems
to me. He takes care of practical things; he doesn't believe in talking things over . . .

Therapist: Well, if in our meeting we were also to tend to more
practical things, maybe your husband would feel more
inclined to come? And you wouldn't feel so alone with
your problems.

Mother: If you want, I'll try it out. . . .

This short segment, taken from an initial telephone conversation, illustrates briefly some of the points we mentioned
above. Above all, it demonstrates the attempt to create a relationship between the elements provided by the caller and
those that the therapist perceives as informative voids, based
on his past experiences and on the images that these evoke in
him. He may also create relationships based on emotional dis-
sonance in his perception of the way various pieces of the
puzzle fit together or stay unmatched. This is done, for example, through the metaphor of the rooms, which by spatial
representation alludes to the people involved and expands
the participation to include other family actors. Another example is the question of who takes the initiative of going into
the other's room, where their mutual relationship comes into
the scene, and is then extended to the husband's behavior
with implications about the conjugal relationship.

Thus, the therapist seeks to give life and movement to the
description of symptoms presented as crystallized attributes

of the patient. In a parallel way, he seeks to put into motion a series of emotions that can motivate people to engage themselves in a therapeutic relationship in a perspective that differs from the initial definition of the problem.

With the first telephone call we thus sketch out a scenario of the future therapeutic story. The stronger the emotional stimuli attached to the images evoked by the dialogue, the stronger are our expectations of alliance and dependency needs.

NODAL POINTS AND ALTERNATIVE PATTERNS

We will see how these aspects described above evolve in the course of the first encounter with the Penna family.[6] This family consists of the mother, widowed 15 years ago, and her eight children—two daughters and six sons—the youngest being 17 years old (see Figure 8.1, p. 161, genogram of the Penna family). The family presents from the beginning with a facade of respect and honesty that seems to come directly from the image of the dead father, a generous and good man who left in everyone a void that cannot be filled. Since his death, his importance and stature have become as great as his remoteness, while a series of substitute fathers have attempted to fill the void. Dino, 22 years old, is the identified patient who alternates between periods of great passivity (staying at home for days doing nothing) and brief episodes of running away, which usually end with police intervention and the return home of the prodigal son.

We will focus on a short sequence that illustrates how a therapeutic rapport is established, based on how the therapist uses his perceptions. The family is arranged in a circle, presenting an image of solidarity and passive expectation. The spatial distribution of the participants and the preceding telephone contacts with one of the children suggest a particular assignment of roles.

---

[6]The progress of this family's therapy is presented at length in Chapter 8.

Therapist: (facing the family) You look like a platoon, you must tell me quickly who you are! . . . Who's the one I talked to?

Lucio: To me!

Therapist: Are you the father?

Lucio: (decisively) No!

Therapist: Acting as father?

Lucio: (less sure) Yes!

Therapist: I understand, you're the one who functions as father! And who functions as mother?

Mother: I'm the mother!

Therapist: Oh, you're the mother . . . so you're in your own role. Are you sure that you only act as mother and he as father, or do you act as both father and mother?

Mother: I've been both father and mother, now . . .

Therapist: For how many years?

Mother: For 12 years—in September it will be 12 years since my husband died.

In a previous publication (Andolfi & Angelo, 1981), analyzing an analogous way for the therapist to proceed, we stressed how such sequences are grasped as "nodal points"[7] of the family's relational plot, displaying aspects ignored until then by the various members of the group. To place ourselves in another perspective, let's examine what happens under the rubric of joining. We can say that from the first moment, the therapist seeks to make contact, to enter into the world of his interlocutors, and to see their world through their eyes or their presumed feelings, but reaching for levels that may pass unobserved by individual family members.

---

[7]By "nodal points" we mean communicative redundancies, often verbal or paraverbal, usually ignored by the family, which are available for the construction of a relational map. These are noted by the therapist, who uses them to punctuate in a different way both the relationships among the various participants and what happens in the session.

For example, in the preceding dialogue the therapist's question, "Are you the father?" which appears bizarre and senseless, is actually the final product of a whole series of perceptions and considerations that have activated a world and its associated images in the therapist. This is the world of social conventions in which the one who takes the initiative to take a sick family member for treatment is usually one of the two parents. Whoever does it in a parent's place, therefore, assumes a parent's role. This is what happens to the child in this situation who has made the first telephone contact with the therapist and to whom the therapist now asks his question.

At this point we can observe two details: (1) The therapist has introduced a perception and has attached a meaning to it which originates from his own experience. (2) However, the therapist has forced himself also to *attend* to something that was already present in the other person's relational experience and gave him a "label." That is, the therapist has *selected* an experience that perhaps did not have a name and was kept "to one side," which in his judgment has an emotional value relevant for the child. These two aspects of the therapeutic intervention are always simultaneously present like the two faces of the double-headed Janus: the predominance of one or the other depends on the situation at hand.

The most important element, which is often neglected, is that what is observed must represent something emotionally meaningful to the person, through which he or she feels that the therapist has selected a relevant affective experience; and therefore the individual feels the possibility of being understood and of sharing with the therapist a part of his or her own world. Given that such a shared reality is the result of a series of interactions that take place within a process, there must be accommodations on both sides—that is, adaptations of the actual image each constructs of the other—in an attempt to arrive at an identification acceptable to both.

That is what helps to keep the dialogue going when, after Lucio's negative response to the first question, the therapist adds, "The acting father?"—receiving an affirmative, though hesitant, response. The same procedure occurs soon after in the interactions with the mother, to whom the new definition (" . . . or do you act as both mother and father?") is proposed only after the one given by herself. Even here the question probably touches on experiences of suffering, perhaps never expressed within the family and related to the need to fill a parental void.

We are focusing especially on the subject of joining, because we consider it to be fundamental for a good outcome of therapy. In fact, good outcome implies joining because it is identified with the capacity to grasp the present psychological conditions of the members of the system, and consequently, the problems and the conditions that are related to them. As we will demonstrate, joining is enacted essentially through individuals, who each act as a medium for the rest of the family, and who can be switched from time to time. Although in the past we emphasized predominantly definitions and interventions concerning the whole family, viewing interventions with individuals as not very "relational," a reexamination of our conversations from therapy sessions and a different punctuation of these make us notice that the role of the individual in the construction of the relationship and in the creation of moments of high emotional tension is decisive. The emotion always occurs in situations that involve the individual with others. At the same time, such situations concern his most intimate experiences and how they both structure the relationship and are modified within it.

The therapist therefore constructs a relationship with the family through his rapport with its different components and, at the same time, through the way in which he unites their diverse experiences, giving them a meaning in a comprehensive frame. The construction of the relationship through the individual and the way in which it is enacted also explains how to make the *supportive actions* that must always accompany every prospective attack on dysfunctional behavior, as we will see in what follows.

To enter into the world of one's interlocutor, however, does not mean passively registering its structure: if it was that way, one would have to contradict the statement that has become commonplace, "the map is not the territory." Every type of learning inevitably brings an active structuring of information in the form of connective schemata.

What is apparently a collection of information therefore becomes a means of creating information within the perceptual structure of the interlocutor. This structure is already coded according to a series of values given to the elements contained in it and connected through a network of relationships. Joining constitutes, at the same time therefore, a means of uniting and an instrument of change. To evoke an image or to suggest a definition or a meaning is also to act through these things.

Therapist: (facing Dino, the I.P.) But, wait a minute, you aren't one of the spouses and you aren't one of the kids *(as the other children were defined)*. Who are you?

Dino: (laughing a little) I'm part of the family just like everybody else.

Therapist: But how is it they haven't put you with the kids, and they haven't placed you with the parents?

Dino: Because I'm usually out of the house!

Therapist: I understand! . . . So you're the one in the family who comes and goes!

Dino: Well, before, yes, but now I stay home . . . *(indecisive)*

Therapist: So now you stay more? To check out how Lucio is doing as a father? *(pointing to Lucio, Dino's brother)*

To touch on this aspect of the identified patient's identity and his place in the hierarchy of the family is not only to make contact with one of the most sensitive parts of his problem, but also to invite him to define himself, thus interacting with him and at the same time inviting him to act. This invitation emerges precisely from the fact that information has

been introduced into the patient's world in order to change his perceptual field. If this attempt succeeds (as confirmed by an eventual acceptance of the proposed image), the result strengthens the patient's bond with the therapist by satisfying the request which is implicit in every therapy: to find different answers than those used in the past to resolve the patient's existential problems.

The therapist proposes the appropriate canvas to the family, while slowly constructing the scheme based on his initial impressions, using information received from each member. It is important to emphasize how this alternative scheme is placed as an *intermediate object* with which everyone interacts. It therefore acquires a life of its own, just like a real object, and becomes the third side of the triangle whose other two sides are taken up by the family and the therapist.

THE THERAPEUTIC RELATIONSHIP:
BETWEEN PART AND WHOLE

We have already seen that the therapist, in his role as a new but temporary and highly meaningful link, becomes a prime element for modifying the family schema. Based on this premise and on the impossibility of "entering into the family's past experiences and history," it is possible to *construct a story* with the family in the context of therapy. Within this temporary and "artificial" story, it is possible for the family to learn how to find different meanings for the events and interactions of family life and eventually to try out new alternatives in real life.

In the construction of the therapeutic story, the therapist becomes an integral part of the family, just as the family becomes part of the therapeutic team, to the point that each of them disappears as a separate entity and finds him- or herself in another time and place: the therapeutic system or what we have called *the third planet* (Andolfi & Angelo, 1984).

Change and the proof of change in a certain sense go beyond the therapeutic context. Change depends on the fam-

ily's search for solutions beyond the family, on the degree to which it learns to tie together each individual's conflicts in a new way in therapy. What it learns is above all a way of working rather than specific solutions to substitute for the preceding ones. Just as the therapist, after learning a method, can apply it to an endless variety of therapeutic relationships, so can the family apply the method it learns to future problems whenever the family's development requires new adaptations and a different integration of each individual's life and their collective involvement in the same evolving story.

It is precisely in the dynamic balance between being and belonging that the therapist intervenes, as he weaves back and forth from the individual to the family. At such moments, the therapist redirects what emerges from forming a relationship with each person back to their relationships with the other members of the system. This "forming a relationship" with the individual is neither a spontaneous exchange between the two, nor a stable confidential relationship, as in individual psychotherapy. It is more like the situation that develops when the therapist is able to speak to the family through the emotions, sentiments, and silences of one of its members. The therapist reviews the individual's personal problems in order to highlight the shared aspects that they represent for the other members of the system. This twofold action of making contact with an individual and separating quickly thereafter in order to reconnect him to the whole family is comparable to the mechanism of breathing, in which inhaling and exhaling are equally fundamental and complementary. If the therapist secures a reference point by which to orient himself throughout the course of therapy, he will be able to slowly bring into play personal reactions, such as images, moods, and symbols, to establish and develop the therapeutic story. The therapist's observations and intuitions then become elements of exchange and a constant source of information, for which a creative imagination plays a central role (Hutten, 1975).

To illustrate this, we have another excerpt from a session with the Penna family six months later. In the previous session, the therapist had asked the family to find and bring family photographs that included the father. However, on the pretense of a misunderstanding, the family brought mostly pictures of the identified patient (who becomes the subject of everyone's comments) and only a few of other family members.

Lucio: A few days ago, I was thinking that father is never together with us.

Therapist: Was he already dead?

Mother: No, it's just that he never joined us in pictures.

Therapist: But it occurs to me that maybe he was dead before he actually died . . . you talk about him as a ghost to the point that I thought he died earlier. Who was this man, by the way?

Mother: He was a working man. He didn't have any vices, only that if he couldn't afford to buy something, he bought it anyway . . . money slipped through his fingers and he signed bad checks . . . because of this I had arguments with him.

Therapist: What arguments? . . . maybe he was the failure in the family before Dino?

Lucio: Maybe so, because my father didn't like work . . . so much so that he gave it up.

Dino: I remember when my father and my mother fought with each other . . . maybe it influenced a lot of things . . . my mind, my anxiety . . .

Therapist: You're talking about another failure, because Lucio was talking about professional failure. At home was the idea that your dad was a failure denied, or did you talk about it?

Dino: Well, before, I don't know; but after he died we never talked about my father at home.

Therapist: So even for you he was a bit of a ghost?

Dino: It's an empty hole I have in my life, a ghost, something that doesn't exist, but it affects so many things . . .

Therapist: Do you think that the relationship between your dad and your mom was already dead for a long time?

Lucio: (*interrupting*) Well, maybe the answer is yes . . . it had died a long time before.

Therapist: So the children who were born were conceived in the cemetery? (*turning to mother*) Signora, did I bring up something that's too heavy?

Mother: No, go ahead, because my husband always treated me well. His only vice was being a spendthrift. He had mania to buy even when he couldn't.

Therapist: So you've always preferred to keep up a front and sweep all your real problems under the rug—your disappointments, your loneliness, your grudges, your emptiness. . . . Where have they all gone? When did your relationship die?

Mother: After two months of marriage . . . the quarreling started soon after. He knew how to lie, he could talk well. He was a great talker but he couldn't be bothered about anything. He wanted the children, because he was an only child, and so he didn't want his children to be only children, alone in the world like he was. I came from a big family and didn't want them, but meanwhile . . . eight kids and as many abortions.

After six months of therapy, the father, who was as out of reach as a living myth as he was in death, has been reviewed and remade into a completely marginal and rather wretched figure. The therapist, picking up apparently trivial perceptions (e.g., the almost total absence of the father in the pictures that the family selected to show him), now has a new perspective of the therapeutic drama and its function. Taking the death of the father as a nodal point, his importance and meaning have become restructured through a progression of images: "he was already dead . . . he was dead before he died . . . father a failure . . . father a ghost . . . a dead relationship . . . children of the cemetery. . . . " This allows each family member to progress from an image of the father as an "idealized ghost" to the feeling of an absence or void, which they have denied all along. The theme of failure, centered for a long time on Dino's symptomatic behavior, grows like an oil slick.

We can see throughout the dialogue how the therapist weaves back and forth from each individual to the family as a whole. The point of departure is always the person with his feelings and what is attributed to him, which all becomes quickly reconnected to the rest of the group as the therapist searches for a collective meaning. This search becomes more meaningful the more it succeeds in placing a boundary or an intermediary between the components of the therapeutic story: the individual, the family, and the therapist. An example is the therapist's repetitive emphasis on the existential void which has always existed in the family and which he symbolized as a father already metaphorically dead, well before the real event. The image of the ghost is meaningful for Dino in providing him with a multifaceted symbol, through which he identifies with the privations of his father; just as it is for the rest of the family in placing different connotations on the grief that characterizes the family myth, through a picture of father different from what was officially handed down. And finally, it is meaningful for the therapist, who introduces his own image, drawing from his personal experience, as a creative response to the stimulus produced by the family interactions and his participation in the therapeutic story. When he translates the perceived sense of emptiness and gives it a name (ghost, death, cemetery), the therapist becomes aware of the family's implicit request for him to be a substitute father; and he can decide how to respond to it. When he *gives them an answer* and acknowledges the emptiness and need in each member of the family, he agrees to be the "temporary father" of the family, in this way offering each of them the chance to shed the role attributed to them until now.

The multiple aspects that the relational and existential death of this family takes on allow us to distinguish which of them concern the individual's interactions and which represent the enigmatic relationships of the others, of which the individual is an unwilling carrier. The father's absence or his ineffectiveness, masked by his superficial definition as a good and upright person, is a problem which Dino, the identified patient, continually had to confront, seeking out someone who would respond to his old requests for dependency and for guidance and help him to find alternative answers. What he cannot come to feel as his own, however, is the relational void created only a few months after his parents' marriage. This was an experience that does not belong to him and that he cannot therefore symbolize. In the "relational script" that he has internalized, his parents' relationship remains an enigma. In spite of this, to his mother he is a product of her failed marriage and is the carrier of a series of meanings that reevoke that failure through his symptoms.

It is only when the therapist redirects such meanings to their original context, helping the mother express all the bitterness and disappointment that she carried inside her for years, that the patient can see from the outside for the first time what he was carrying around inside himself[8] and to whom it really belonged. In this way, a new story is constructed in therapy in which a map is proposed. This map is

---

[8]We have spoken about the patient's situation only to show how to form a relationship with the individual and his emotional problems in order to reconnect them quickly to family relationships and to the meaning that they assume in this context. Similarly, we could naturally have done it with any member of the family, as one discovers in the course of therapy, even if, from time to time, we select mostly one person as a "portal of entry" into the system.

not the same as the boundaries of the individual members of the family, because it attempts to redefine their respective functions and personal spaces. The therapist represents a new link who uses his imagery to act as a catalyst in the search for new relational journeys that seek to give a different sense to the family story as a whole.

CHAPTER 2

Triangles and Trigenerational Networks

THE TRIANGLE AS A UNIT OF OBSERVATION

Our growing interest in the importance of placing the individual within a system, especially the family, is a result of the development of our relational approach, analogous to the study of perceptual processes. In these studies, the individual was initially considered to be completely passive, his cognitive structures shaped by external "impressions," without any active participation in the perception of his environment. When it was discovered that perceptual processes are actively "shaped" by the subject, the external world was no longer a series of objective data but the product of interactions between the elements that constitute it and the perceptual activity of the person who constructs it (Bruner, Olver, & Greenfield, 1966; Neisser, 1967). This activity is structured over time by learning processes; as a result, the data of one's personal history assume special prominence through emotional experiences connected to them.

If this theory is applied to the family situation, it follows that the individuals who participate in this situation are not products completely determined by the system to which they belong, but actively converge to define its characteristics and balances. Each individual, therefore, is a potential source of entry of new stimuli into the system. This has led some authors (Cronen et al., 1982; Liotti, 1983) to hypothesize a continual circular exchange between a family system and its individual members, hierarchically arranged and whose contents reciprocally influence each other.

The various triangular hypotheses of relationships that have been formulated (Bowen, 1966; Coppersmith, 1983; Haley, 1959, 1976, 1977; Ricci & Selvini Palazzoli, 1984; Selvini Palazzoli et al., 1980b) have been brilliantly synthesized by Hoffman (1981). In this chapter we are interested in exploring a particular theme: the resolution of conflict in triadic relationships and the influence that this conflict may have on the process of personal individuation.

Let us take, for example, the most common triadic situation: a child and his two parents. The child has often been described as functioning to *detour the conflict* between the parents. This has brought out two aspects. First, this function is protective when it operates as an "outflow channel" for tension between the parents. And this function actively opposes all of the couple's attempts to define directly the conflicting motives in their relationship, in a dialogue for the two of them, without intermediaries or allies. Giving up the use of intermediaries, in fact, would take away the importance of the child's role as a meaningful third person and would place him in a position of relative isolation, preventing him from drawing strength from an alliance with either one of the parents. It would deprive him, moreover, of his function as regulator controlling the fear of disrupting family bonds from the eruption of violent emotions.

We want to emphasize another important aspect, about the *element of novelty* introduced by the appearance of a third person in a conflict between two others. The third person adds a new dimension to the interaction which enables alliances to occur and a dialogue of inclusion or exclusion between them, as described by many authors (Bowen, 1966; Coppersmith, 1983; Haley, 1959, 1976, 1977; Minuchin, 1974; Ricci & Selvini

Palazzoli, 1984; Scheflen, 1972; Selvini Palazzoli et al., 1980b; Weakland, 1976; Zuk, 1968). A third person can also be a stimulus for the emergence of hidden individual resources and for the evolution of the system. This is possibly due to the fact that in triadic interaction, in contrast to dyadic interaction,[1] each of the participants can stay and watch what happens between the other two.

In this way, while a child is interacting with one of his parents, he gives the other parent an opportunity to know both of them better by being an observer of their interactions. From this position, the observing parent can collect information from each of them which is useful to him or her when he or she, in turn, is involved in an interaction with one of them. He or she will be able to understand which emotions rouse the others, which gestures and expressions accompany them, what irritates them, what pleases them, and so on, confirming previous impressions or discovering surprise aspects that he or she had not noticed before. This opportunity offers itself, from time to time, to each member of the triangle, whenever he or she finds himself or herself in a position as observer of what happens between the other two.

Triadic interactions also have other possibilities. If, for example, father and mother argue because they have different opinions on a particular matter, the child can intervene in the discussion by adopting a less controversial attitude and defusing the interaction when it becomes too intense. A parent can do the same thing when the spouse argues with their child. Seeing how another person deals with the kind of difficulties one is facing helps one to learn behaviors and to shape the potential tensions in a way that makes situations more tolerable and productive. Each member of the triad can thus take on, in critical periods of the family's development, the func-

---

[1]We are thinking here of *interactions*, that is, exchanges that occur in reality and that can develop between two or more people, in contrast to *relationships*, which we define as structures, whose basic unity is represented by the triangle.

tion of a *model* by containing and mediating the tensions that exist between the other two. In this perspective, the presence of a third party becomes important *to facilitate intimacy*, providing the support necessary for the development and integration of mutual feelings. This is also important during changes in the family life cycle—after a period of separation, for example, when support is needed for working through the loss. Another example is when children leave home. The mediation of one of the parents is often crucial to ease anxiety that could hinder the child's leaving and to provide an alternative support.

TRIGENERATIONAL TRIANGLES

If, in agreement with many authors (Boszormenyi-Nagy & Spark, 1973; Bowen, 1978; Carter & McGoldrick, 1980; Framo, 1982; Scabini, 1984; Walsh, 1982; Whitaker, 1982; Williamson, 1981), we add a third dimension to our field of observation by placing triangular relationships on a trigenerational plane, we can pull together more complex aspects of current relationships. When the individuals involved are seen through their

> specific ways of interacting with their own trigenerational family, they appear as complex entities, full of contradictions and of conflicts. For an observer, however, they become tools for understanding the internal world of the individuals when trying to grasp the implicit links between current behaviors and experiences and past feelings, which would otherwise be perceived as fragmentary and unrelated. (Andolfi & Angelo, 1985a, p. 20)

We will try to explain our point of view better with a diagram, which illustrates how a complex relational network is constructed by linking various relational triangles (see Figure 2.1).

If we refer to a couple W and H (wife and husband), where D represents a daughter and M and F represent the mother and father of the wife, we can see that the wife finds herself at a crossroad where two planes intersect. Her position in the

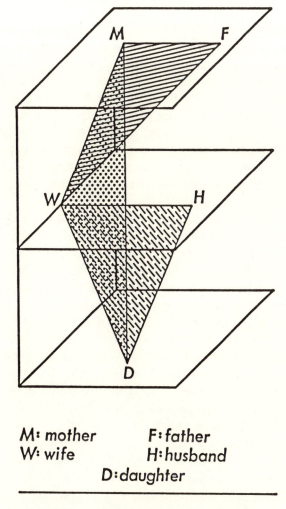

M: mother   F: father
W: wife   H: husband
          D: daughter

Figure 2.1.   Three-generational triangles.

generational hierarchy of her family of origin places her on a vertical plane. The horizontal plane is constituted by her marital relationship and other possible bonds (with siblings, for example), which have been omitted for the sake of simplicity. The relational networks that emerge from the diagram can be broken down to a series of many triangles in which the sides are occupied by different people at different times. The bonds that these triangles comprise convey many requests. Although these demands originate in single relationships, they seek fulfillment even in distant relationships if they were not satisfied in the original one.

For example, if the wife has a difficult relationship with her own mother or with her husband, who fail to meet her emotional demands, these demands will probably be redirected to the daughter. The daughter's relationship with the mother is therefore complicated by the presence of two superimposed components: one which involves her directly and another in which she becomes the mediator of a demand initially directed at someone else (her maternal grandmother or her father, to limit ourselves to only two triangles). Therefore, she must resolve the ambiguity arising from the simultaneous presence of these two levels and her dilemma about the relationships between the people involved in the other two sides of the triangle if she wants to free herself.

In order to illustrate this further, let us consider the case of Lisa Moscati, a woman of 50, married for 25 years, who has suffered depressive episodes for some time. Both Lisa, who is an only child, and her husband, who is four years older, were raised in families that discouraged the expression of emotion. In his family of origin the husband explains that this was "because there were more important things to do," such as struggling with day-to-day problems. In her family of origin, Lisa was taught by her rigid and introverted mother that emotional expression was a sign of weakness. These attitudes reflected what each of them had actually seen their parents do to each other, and what were now faithfully reproduced in their own marriage. Lisa, especially, has become convinced that the failure of her marriage is partly due to her inability to be affectionate, for which her husband often reproaches her. Each of them feels rejected and not accepted by the partner, which is compensated by their hopes for the future satisfaction of unmet needs from their daughter.

This couple has a daughter who is now 24. Lisa, who has always been a rather cold and authoritarian mother, now expresses a need for affection from her daughter. Lisa was unable to express this need in her family of origin. She now expects to receive from her daughter what she was not able to get from her own mother and from her husband. When Lisa complains about her relationship with her husband, her daughter listens to her attentively, seeking to console her and encouraging her to be patient, but the daughter nonetheless maintains a conflictual relationship with her.

For her part, in spite of numerous partners, the daughter has never had a stable relationship. She, too, is incapable of expressing the affection that she was always denied. In her interactions with her mother she finds herself in a contradictory position. She would like to be dependent on her mother at just the very moment when her mother wants to depend on her.

Lisa's attempt to find an answer to her own lack of feelings (and her depression represents the failure of that attempt) is therefore reproduced in a process of delegation (Stierlin, 1978), which transmits the quest for the satisfaction of the original needs from one generation to the next.

FAMILY COORDINATES

Accordingly, understanding the individual and his developmental processes is facilitated by constructing an observational schema which permits us to see his present behavior as relational metaphors, or as indirect signals of past needs and emotional involvements that manifest themselves concretely in present relationships (Andolfi & Angelo, 1985a).

Thus, either verbal or nonverbal information about how the relationship between father and son is currently expressed (which we will call second and third generations, respectively) also contains implicit and complementary information about how the parent currently perceives past interactions between himself and his own father (i.e., between the second and first generations). The complexity increases if we connect this to the more abstract, ideal images about how to be a father and a son. Such images are incorporated with greater or lesser intensity by each of us in our own family and cultural contexts, and at times they become personal codes for behavior.

Let us try to explain this better with a clinical example. Mr. Vianini is talking in the session of his extreme difficulty in being accepted as a father by his only son, Marco, who is 13. He has reached the point of fearing that the boy does not need him anymore: "He's always playing videogames with his friends or he stays for hours with his little computer" (which was a gift from his father!).

These problems appear irrelevant to Marco, who wears headphones attached to a portable tape player which he uses to include or exclude himself during moments of emotional intensity in the session. Marco describes his father as totally unavailable to play with him. Both father and son present the situation with a complete lack of confidence in the possibility of change, mixed with a deep sense of bitterness about giving up such an important relationship. Most of all, the father communicates a considerable impasse, a sort of paralysis, in approaching his son. This paralysis seems to say much more, and on different levels, than just his difficulty of feeling like a father to his 13-year-old son. It is perhaps by getting a better focus on the specific and concrete aspects of the interactions between the two that we can visualize the play of relational exclusions and overinclusions, which are much more complex than is usual between generations.

We must then enter the paralysis of the father, break it down into its various components, and amplify the frame. Let us start with the boy. The boy recounts how he tries to include his father in his play. The conclusion always seems to be the same: as soon as he "sees" that his father is annoyed or detached, he gives up and leaves the room. During this sequence, and in the course of the subsequent sessions, the boy looks for strength and reassurance from his mother, on whom his eyes are glued.

Something similar occurs in another session, at which the paternal grandfather, an old man of 85, is present. The father refers to always having been shy with his father, with whom he could never play and had never talked, and how he had always turned to his mother. Discussing this is a great effort for Mr. Vianini, who begins to stutter when talking about himself at the age of 11. As for the grandfather, he is fed up with "looking into so many useless details, when life is the same for everybody. And these are certainly not the real problems of life. If anything, the real problem is health!" In the course of the session, a kind of rule emerges about the family: well-being at work always compensated sickness at home. The grandfather's wife had been an invalid in bed for 25 years before dying. However, the business which the grandfather still manages and where his four children work, including Marco's father, has always been an essential lifeline for this family, providing all kinds of compensations for each of them at key times in their development, depending on their emotional needs. These compensations have such an important function that none of them, beginning with the grandfather, is capable of freeing him/herself from this lifeline which has become vital. Not to include the company in the father's paralysis, or more generally, in the outlook that has guided the life of the Vianini family, would be to leave out an important piece of their relational mosaic.

Until now we have been discussing relationships that move up and down the vertical axis. Now, let us see what happens when the vertical axis, which we can define as the parental plane, encounters the horizontal axis, which we will call the marital plane.

In other words, our relational horizon extends and expands if we place the couple's space in a broader territory, in which marital relations become the meeting point and the synthesis of two different family histories. In a certain sense, we think that a newly formed couple fits into a river that draws streams from the present and the future, based on their own expectations and those of previous generations. With this in mind, we can observe how a person looks for and brings out adult parts in his or her partner to establish a mutual relationship (Wynne, 1984); or if the horizontal axis becomes weighed down with compensatory obligations towards parents or children, which have not developed harmoniously on the vertical axis over time. In the latter case, using the model of complementary unmet needs that influence the selection of a partner (Boszormenyi-Nagy & Spark, 1973), we can think about the recovery of one's own generational space as a rediscovery of the individual self.

Returning to the Vianini family case, we may ask, for example, what made the wife marry a man 15 years older than herself. Is it related to the fact that her father left her mother to marry a much younger woman and move to another country, breaking all ties with his own children? We may also ask what has moved Mr. Vianini to reconnect his wife with her father, while he seems to be totally incapable of reconnecting with his own father, who has become identified with the walls of his company.

BELONGING AND SEPARATION

Everything we have said so far addresses the problem of enlarging the immediate context for observing the symptom, extending the observation from the symptom-bearer to his significant relationships. This raises further questions. One of these questions concerns the elements that ensure the maintenance and the development of these relationships. Another is, how does one construct the meanings attributed to these elements?

The problems of belonging and separation occur throughout the family life cycle. Union and separation seem to proceed step in step and to develop in a circular process. We move apart at the prospect of new unions, so that over time each new union and every successiv₂ separation that follows should be more differentiated than the previous ones. In order to meet in a more satisfying way, first we must move toward a way of relating in which each of the participants can define his or her own personal space (Whitaker & Keith, 1981). Separation is really a process that can last most of one's life without ever being completed. Quite commonly in therapy, if this process is blocked we notice that the behavior of a mother or father is radically transformed in the presence of one of his or her own parents, so that he or she suddenly acts and feels inadequate. This occurred, for example, to Mr. Vianini, who began to stutter in front of his father, recalling how he was at 11 years of age, replaying on the vertical axis the same difficulty and embarrassment that he has with his son.

The more a relationship is based on satisfying the basic needs of protection and security, the stronger is the bond that develops and the greater is the potential danger of any situation that threatens the bond.[2] One tends to react initially to such a situation with hostility towards the people who endanger the relationship and later to protect it in any way possible.

While all this is clear enough regarding the relationship between two people, what happens is less obvious when it takes place within the family network. In fact, even in the stable dyad between mother and son, a third element is always present, either on the horizontal plane (in relationships with the father and other family members) or on the vertical plane (in those between the mother and her family of origin). Therefore, the current experience of the bond between two people is influenced by other historical bonds which are not

---

[2]Bowlby (1969, 1973, 1980) dedicated most of his career to the study of the child's "attachment" to his mother and has described in detail what happens when this bond is endangered by periods of separation of various lengths or becomes interrupted by mourning. His work has recently taken into consideration not only the first years of life, but also the adult years, with the description of precise phases in the development of grief following the loss of a loved one.

always visible. This combination of current and historical experience shapes the expectations that require satisfaction in
the relationship. This helps us understand why the more a
bond survives with unmet needs, the more it tends to be repeated and unchanged in new relationships.

Mr. Ferro, a man of 50, who works as a laborer in a factory,
has been married for many years to a younger woman. They
have three daughters. The oldest daughter suffers from a severe phobic-obsessive disorder that compels her to stay home.
There she is attended by her mother who has given up her
own social life to be a slave to her and now complies with her
every wish. The patient's symptoms threaten the close relationship between her father and her paternal grandmother.
Mr. Ferro's mother is a very authoritarian woman who has
stopped her daily visits to her son's house because she is distressed by her granddaughter's rituals. In fact, this has caused
the grandmother's first absence from the patient's family,
bringing some relief to the mother who always felt invaded
by her mother-in-law in the running of her home. The father
has remained, nonetheless, very attached to his mother,
whom he worships and visits frequently.

In the following excerpt from the second session, the relationships between the father and his mother and with his
wife and daughters are explored.

Therapist: (*turning to the father*) Have you always appreciated
    your mother's authority? Because you speak of her with
    such admiration . . .
Father: Yes, because she kept the family on its feet. Maybe my
    father was a very decent man, but my mother was one
    step ahead of my father.
Therapist: Do you know that your mother has always made
    your wife's life difficult?
Father: Yes.
Therapist: Did you think that in time it might get better or
    were you sure that things couldn't change?

Father: Well I . . . used to say, "It's the sick love that a mother has for her son." I thought that anything my wife could do for my mother wouldn't have worked out, because . . . I have always divided my love: one part for my wife and another for my mother.

Therapist: (*pointing to the father's body*) Which was the part for your wife—the right or the left, the upper part or the lower part?

Father: Let's say the left, the side of the heart . . . because we were engaged for seven years and married for 20 . . . I've loved her, haven't I?

Therapist: And which part did you give to your mother, if you put your feelings there (*indicating the wife*)?

Father: Well, I gave my feelings to my wife and I gave my mother my right hand, because if my mother needs me at any time, she calls and I go. I support her with my right hand, if you want to put it that way (*he makes a fist and holds the muscles of his right arm, in a forceful motion*) . . . because my mother gave me a lot.

Therapist: (*facing the wife*) Of those who are left in the family, who replaced your husband's right arm for you—the part that he gave to his mother?

Mother: Well, partly all three daughters . . .

Therapist: But which one gave you the most support?

Mother: Ornella (*the patient*), because she resented this situation the most.

This excerpt helps us understand that bonds are never limited to two people at a time (such as husband-mother, husband-wife, wife-daughter), but involve different triangles at the same time. In every subsystem of this family, one can in fact see how a specific relationship is potentially threatened by the tensions that exist between one of the members of the relationship and another family member. The effort to maintain a bond is inevitably an effort to keep the system together, in the attempt to contain its tensions.

Taking the father of the identified patient as our central point of reference, we can see how maintaining a strong link with his mother means not only acknowledging his moral obligations (Boszormenyi-Nagy & Spark, 1973) towards her and providing what she lacks (a strong and protective man), but also maintaining a model of relationships by which he has constructed his own sense of security and his emotional relationships with women.

From the beginning, Mr. Ferro's wife had to face this *imprint of needs*[3] in her partner, whose rigidity, emotional debts, and negative experiences of separation and loss (e.g., the premature death of his father) have rendered change and autonomy too threatening for him and his mother.

Mrs. Ferro's husband, on the other hand, responding to the normal needs of adult independence and to have his own family, sought a compromise between opposing needs by taking the most obvious and common solution. He tried to "sit on the fence," going out of his way to reconcile his gratifying and reassuring relationships in complementary ways. This has made it unavoidable for him to fight to maintain the apparently irreconcilable bonds with his mother and with his wife.

The same type of problem faces Ornella, the identified patient, whose disturbed behavior serves as "glue" for her father, her mother, and her grandmother. Paradoxically, how-

---

[3]By the *imprint of needs* we are indicating how the unsatisfied needs of relationships with significant family members are stamped onto each person. This makes the demand to satisfy these needs remain always in the present, with the individual continually seeking solutions in other relationships in order to compensate for the original "absence." These "stand-ins" will almost always be inadequate to satisfy the expectations placed on them due to their only partial similarity with the people who "ought" to satisfy them (for example, a partner cannot be the father or the brother who is sought).

This notion was anticipated by the pioneering American psychologist, William James (1952): " . . . in the one-sided development of civilized life, it happens that the timely age goes by in a sort of starvation of objects, and the individual then grows up with gaps in his psychic constitution which future experiences can never fill" (p. 737).

ever, her actions keep grandmother away from the family's daily life. In this family, each person has learned to be a mediator of opposing needs in order to safeguard his or her own identity and the others' and to keep the system in balance.

At this point, we must pose a question which we will try to answer in the following chapters: What tools does the therapist have to facilitate movement in the family that will lead to growth? And what is the therapist's position in regard to the network of relationships within the family itself?

Many elements place the therapist in a special position with the members of the family. One of the most important, even if it is taken for granted, is the uneven attribution of *authority* and *power*. It seems, in any case, that the operations that the therapist performs are comparable to those carried out by the various family members. The therapist defines different triangles at different times, either by inserting himself in them as a third party or by observing triangular configurations from his external position. In doing this, the therapist is nonetheless in a position of greater freedom compared to the others, because, coming with a different family story, he brings with him a different imprint of needs. That is, he does not necessarily have to support or protect this or that member of the family; neither does he have to protect at any cost the bonds that maintain his own identity. Even when his own story is comparable to that of the patient, we assume that he has already found different solutions, at least for himself.[4]

---

[4]The usefulness of working in a team lies precisely in the possibility for the group behind the mirror to orient the therapist to his position and to the consistency of his interventions and to rescue him from overly involved emotional situations.

CHAPTER 3

Provocation and Holding in Therapy

ON THE CONCEPT OF THERAPEUTIC PROVOCATION

To begin to respond to the question raised in the last chapter—that is, What tools does the therapist have to facilitate movement in the family leading to growth?—we will elaborate the concept of provocation as described in our last book (Andolfi et al., 1983). Provocation has commonly been understood as the verbal or nonverbal behavior, mostly intentional, of challenging the family system, which the therapist engages in order to modify the rules of the family's functioning.

This definition has led to both misunderstanding and prejudice related to the concept of challenge as *confrontation*. The most serious misunderstanding is the notion that *to provoke means only to attack*. This has led many therapists to believe that the more they make people feel uncomfortable, the greater the therapeutic effect. This is somewhat like using electric cattle prods on disturbed and self-destructive people to get their attention and to shock them into behaving more appropriately. Those who have followed this line of thinking have not grasped a fundamental element of the therapeutic provocation. That is, provocation must constantly be accompanied by a *supporting* action, through which the person in the system who feels his or her defenses or role attacked can simultaneously perceive that the therapist has understood his or her underlying problem and the difficulties that it creates for that individual. In order for provocation to be therapeutic it must be accompanied by a joining attitude, that is, it must succeed in transmitting that the therapist is standing by the system while he is attacking it. Illustrative examples of this harmonious way of integrating provocation and support are amply presented in the clinical work of Ackerman (1966, 1970a), Minuchin (1974), Minuchin and Fishman (1981), Napier and Whitaker (1978), Whitaker and Keith (1981), and Farrelly and Brandsma (1974).

Another misunderstanding comes from failing to grasp the distinction between the apparent goal and the real goal of provocation. Provocation is usually transmitted to the system through an individual. Although the individual may appear to be the only target at which provocation is directed, we want to stress that we are always referring to individuals *within a system.* If we provoke a member of the family, we do so while the others are present. In this context, the contents and the intention of the action are also communicated to the others. This is even more obvious in cases where the therapist turns intentionally towards one person in order to speak to someone else, pretending to communicate only with the first person.

This takes us back to what we have said about the triangular structure of every basic relationship. If provocation is a kind of relationship, it must involve at least three components—the therapist, the person to whom the provocation is directed, and a third party. The therapist positions himself at one side of the triangle when he provokes the patient (who is on the second side) to confront the images that the therapist suggests or to discuss the relationships that bind him with other members of the system. When the real person being discussed is absent or when he is part of the past, these images constitute "the third side," as we will see further on. The other participants of the relationship who are present in the session are called, in turn, to occupy the third side. In this way, there is a succession of triangular configurations, connected in different ways, which the therapist enters and leaves in the course of therapy. He enters when he interacts with one of the participants, placing another participant in the observer's position; and leaves at the point where he takes the place of the observer, prompting the second participant to interact with the first one. It is only the position of observer, moreover, that allows the "decentering" necessary for a change of perspectives.

Concerning the idea of *provocativeness*, what is easy to grasp is how the behavior of a person can at times be highly provocative, testing a whole series of rules or prohibitions that are imposed by the situation in which the individual finds himself and seeking to evoke a *reaction* from those close to him. What is more difficult to appreciate is that the concept of provocativeness is a relative concept, which originates in the interaction of several components. Take, for example, this therapeutic situation: a mother is speaking with the therapist, while her adolescent son sits in silence, with his head bowed, staring into empty space with a "neutral" expression on his face. Her husband, completely uninvolved, looks around the room, apparently indifferent to what is being discussed. At a certain point the therapist asks the mother a question which touches on intimate aspects she has never discussed: "How long have you felt alone with your loneliness?" The mother remains perplexed, looks around, sees her husband sitting apart from her, then her son, and finally the therapist again, in a new light. She hesitates for a long time and then states, embarrassed, that she prefers not to respond. The husband shifts around in his chair and accentuates his uninvolvement; the son crouches lower into himself. The mother's reaction, accompanied by an increase of tension in the room, indicates that the question was taken by her and by the others as a provocation. But where and on what level is the provocation in the sequence we have just described? Is it in the question posed by the therapist, in the son's attitude, or in the behavior of the husband? Or in all three of these elements together?

In effect, each of these is important in shaping the response, because each contributes to outlining the context in which the question is placed and therefore in defining the meaning. The question is provocative not only because it touches on the person's sensitivity, but also because it reveals his or her relationships, disturbing the delicate balance made up of everything that binds him or her to the others. A question is provocative when it creates movement in a static situation—that is, when a reevaluation leads the individual to question the meaning attributed to an experience. The individual can now perceive past aspects of the experience that were ignored or avoided and which require new attributions and choices to be made.

Which sensitive part of the mother does the therapist's question strike? Probably the fact that she has been used to masking her own loneliness with an attitude of self-sufficiency. To speak of her loneliness in such a direct way is a little like removing her mask and forcing her to reflect on the relationships that are behind it. However, it is also true that the mother's attitude works in a complementary way with the others' attitudes and is somehow reinforced by their apparent detachment. This is what ensures the equilibrium of the system that serves to cover up feelings. The therapist's provocation, apparently directed only at the mother, is therefore a provocation of the interactions between the father and the son, implicitly highlighting their detached attitude, and a provocation of the system as a whole, which emphasizes the dysfunctional patterns. At the same time, along with provocation, we can observe a joining action when the therapist touches the loneliness of the mother.

From another viewpoint, we can note, however, that what is provocative is not only the therapist's question to the mother, but also the silent "stillness" of the son and, in a more obvious way, the uninvolvement of the father. What to consider stimulus or response depends on the punctuation that is given to a relational sequence. What is provocative or not can be defined, consequently, only within the relationship.

One of the first possible considerations is that an indispensable corollary of a provocative action is the presence of rules of the relationship, namely, the norms that provocation brings out. The rules of the relationship are not only norms attached to external relations and shared by others, but also "intrapsychic" norms that enact internal scenarios.

The behavior is not provocative if it does not test the kinds of responses and relationships in the system regarding the particular component that is addressed by the provocation. This sparks a chain reaction upsetting the equilibrium, largely independent of the original spark, but each event linked to the other.

Here it is possible to introduce a further distinction. The connotation of challenge is usually the result of resistance by people who feel unbalanced by the provocation. This happens when aspects of relationships or of people that are very conflictual or in contrast with the person's self-image are touched upon and are revealed to outsiders. In these cases, those affected react by distancing themselves or by opposing the image or the definition proposed. In the case at hand, the mother's embarrassment is already indicative of her resistance to examine an emotional experience that is the synthesis of a series of emotional ups and downs in her unsatisfactory relationships. The amplification of this experience, which is a consequence of every successful provocation, tends to melt frozen states such as "loneliness" into more fluid processes. That this process involves the father and the son is demonstrated by the fact that in response to the therapist's question, *the father moves nervously in his chair, enhancing his detachment, and the son crouches down further into himself.*

But it is not always like this. There are situations in which the people and the system they are a part of do not resist the provocation but, after some initial disorientation, support what is said, collaborating in the creation of a new perceptual context, as we will see shortly in the case of Jimmy. One could say that in this case, provocation, by being attached to the novelty of the stimulus introduced into the family's perception, does not become incompatible with it. Whether provocation is complied with or elicits resistance, it transmits information because it introduces new elements into the therapist's perception, partly restructuring his view of the individual or family. This is possible only in a perspective that takes into consideration the whole therapeutic system and not just the family in treatment. Only in this way can the therapist be seen as *the creative element*, which introduces new stimulus into a repetitive pattern.

The difference between the first case and the one that follows is only a difference in intensity. The intensity of the provocation is directly proportional to the rigidity of the rules it encounters. Attitudes are more or less provocative depending on the greater or lesser elasticity of the value systems and the reference points held by those whom the attitudes concern.

Another consideration is that the validity and the quality of the rules are relative to the context. What meets with indifference in one context is charged with tension in another. To speak of the mother's loneliness takes on a special meaning in a context where her quick, pressured way of speaking is in shrill contrast to the silence and disinterest of the others. The context that is created emphasizes the importance of some elements more than others within it. It would have been different if the father or the son had intervened from time to time or had changed their demeanor. What then is provocation?

From what we have said, it is clear that an answer should take into account the factors that condition the very existence of an act of provocation: (a) that it tests or attempts to modify with force the norms or the perceptual and behavioral schemata in relationships; (b) that it encounters a particular rigidity or that it introduces ways of seeing so different as to generate a strong state of tension; (c) that the context favors the display of these elements. All these factors lead to a time and a place in which they are defined. At the same time, we can recognize a time for provocation, in which each element converges to make it more effective. Going back to the previous example, the therapist's question to the mother seems provocative precisely because it is preceded by a context of indifference towards her emotional experiences, as defined by the behavior of the other family members.

Actions that are externally "provocative" may in fact not be experienced that way at all. There is, therefore, a difference between the *intention* to be provocative and really being provocative, even if the external behavior *may seem to be* very provocative. For this reason we must ask the question: What does it mean "to provoke" a family or a system and what can be "provocative" in their interactions?

THE PROCESS OF PROVOCATION: THE CASE OF JIMMY

Based on the premises we proposed, in our opinion being provocative means "touching" elements that are especially emotionally meaningful for family relationships or images or ways of seeing that have become rigid over time. These are the elements that the system and its members seek to maintain unaltered, since those elements represent something that makes these individuals feel vulnerable.

This is clear in the following situation in which the problem concerns an adolescent with behavioral difficulties at school and rebelliousness in the family that have created serious conflicts. The identified patient, Jimmy, sits a little apart from the group with an expression that is both bored and surly, head bowed, while the other family members state the problem. The mother, who is very obese, plays the part of the intermediary and of the family "psychologist." She sits enthroned between the father and Jimmy, as a sort of physical "pillow" between them. The father stays silently above it all. The brother is handicapped, as a consequence of a serious car accident.

Increase in Interpersonal Tensions
in the Session: Compression Phase

The discussion is about the arguments between between father and sons.

Therapist: (facing the patient) And you, Jimmy, do you ever fight with your dad?

Jimmy: Yeah, sometimes.

Therapist: And how do you fight with him?

Jimmy: I just play-fight.

Therapist: Oh, so you don't fight because you're mad at him?

Mother: Yes, I think he is, often . . .

Therapist: Did you ever think you would have preferred another father, rather than him?

Jimmy: (shakes his head, not very convinced)

Therapist: Never? I can't believe it.

Mother: So you don't remember what you told me yesterday or a few days ago?

Jimmy: What?

Mother: Don't you remember that you told me that you hate your father? This is a very strong word to use about your father.

Therapist: Do you mean hatred in the sense of killing him or in the sense of giving him a punch in the face?

Mother: (quoting Jimmy in the first person) "I hate him, he doesn't understand anything I tell him; he doesn't know how to talk to me." This is true as far as I'm concerned, because I know his father has a terrible temper, especially after all the stress he's been having, with Jimmy's problems at school and at home. It's very hard when his father is so busy and then it's difficult for him to know what to do in some situations. He just doesn't have time to stop and think.

Therapist: Who, Jimmy or his dad . . . ? Oh, you're talking about dad, OK. I was talking about Jimmy's hatred towards his dad.

Mother: Jimmy doesn't understand and his dad doesn't understand, they don't understand each other. Jimmy doesn't understand what his dad tries to say or do . . .

Therapist: So you have to play at being the pillow . . .

Mother: That's right, the person in the middle . . .

Therapist: But you play the part of a nice pillow, surely, and this is a good way to keep them apart.

As in the first example, here, too, it is the context of rejection between father and son, with the mother who wears herself out to manage the situation and to act as a "pillow," that prepares and allows the following provocative intervention by the therapist. With his intervention, the therapist seeks to voice the hidden conflict and to emphasize the mother's function, preparing to take a temporary place in the triangle. Soon after, in fact, he asks the mother to move from her seat and places father and son beside each other. The father is asked to show how he can be close to his son and what he does to gain his trust, but each time that the father tries to draw him closer, the son retreats with an increasingly annoyed demeanor.

Therapist: (*facing and referring to Jimmy*) When did you begin to feel that your son was lost to you? How many years ago did you begin to feel that he was no longer interested in your relationship?

Father: Two, maybe three years ago.

Therapist: When was the last time you felt close to him? Can you remember the occasion, a situation, a time?

Father: I think it was when he was eight years old.

Therapist: Can you tell me a story from when you were eight years old, Jimmy? Around the time when you thought that Dad was being a father to you? (*Jimmy pretends to fidget and looks down, hiding his embarrassment.*)

Father: Talk, talk to the doctor!

Jimmy: I don't know.

Therapist: I think you are too preoccupied with thinking of killing him to remember what the situation was like when you still hoped to have a father . . . and now, you are too angry. How can you live with your anger? Did you ever think that you could explode like an overblown balloon that bursts? Boom! (*The patient shakes his head.*) Never? You never thought of it? So Mom has to keep down her weight and you have to keep down your anger and your dad feels like an empty person . . . that's very sad. . . . (*facing Jimmy*) Can you get up? I want to see how tall you are compared to your dad (*Both of them stand and approach each other, without touching, one in front of the other; the father is very embarrassed, Jimmy quickly steps back.*) Who's the stronger one of you two? (*Jimmy doesn't answer.*) So you don't even think that your dad is physically stronger than you are . . . (*Jimmy looks down.*) This is very serious . . . if you don't even think he's stronger than you physically, you must really feel like a little monster. . . . Oh, that's really sad! . . . Did you ever see yourself as a monster? Like this one, see. (*He shows Jimmy a little rubber puppet that he's holding in his hands and that he's been playing with until now, which he squeezes, popping out its eyes and tongue into a grotesque expression.*) See this little monster? It sticks out its eyes, its ears, its mouth. . . . Do you want to play with it? You can take it. (*The patient does not want to take it, but the therapist puts it into his hand, makes him squeeze it, and the puppet sticks out its eyes and ears.*) This is a little monster (*turning to sit down after a brief pause*). This is all too sad. . . . So we have a little monster, a brother who is severely handicapped, a mother who is a chubby psychologist, and a depressed father.

The provocation is initially in the words the therapist uses and which evoke images that condense the tensions that are already part of the context. It begins with the first questions to Jimmy about his negative feelings towards his father, continues with a definition of the mother's function, and increases progressively through the session with mother's displacement and with a direct confrontation between father and son and their definitions. In reality, provocation becomes a process of provocation in which the perception of difference and of separation between parents and children is amplified and exacerbated.

It is exactly the apparently irreversible aspect of the proposed images, related to the theme of separation, that potentiates the tension on which the interventions that follow are based. From the idea of having a different father and from the wish to "punch him," we move on to the patient's more violent and contradictory feelings towards his father ("I think you are too preoccupied with thinking of killing him to remember what the situation was like when you still hoped to have a father"). Then comes the description of his state of tension ("How do you live with your anger? Did you ever think that you could explode like an overblown balloon that bursts? Boom!"), and finally the image that provides something of a synthesis of Jimmy's emotional situation: "You must really feel like a little monster."

It is evident that the situation just described is an example of the kind of provocation that touches on strongly conflictual elements of a relationship, aspects that arouse contrasting emotions. They are fought with silence or the creation of spatial distance, giving up a confrontation that would bare very deep wounds. Provocation aims at breaking the rigidity of this relational structure by increasing the internal pressure which follows a compressive movement (Stanton, 1984). This attempt is reinforced by the use of a metaphorical object, which concretely emphasizes what we have stated. This issue will be taken up again and developed further in Chapter 4.

The next step is for the therapist to create channels that act as safety valves for defusing the tension that is generated in this way. These channels are alternatives for those usually employed, switching the inquiry onto a trigenerational plane.

Channels for Deflecting Tension:
Decompression Phase

Father: My parents split up; I had a hard life when I was small, from the age of 12 I lived on my own . . .

Therapist: What forced you to leave home at the age of 12?

Father: My father . . . I don't know how to say it . . . was the type of guy . . . he never treated me like a son. He treated me really badly, when I was young.

Therapist: Can you give me an idea?

Father: Like I was nobody . . .

Therapist: Like a dog?

Father: Yeah, like a dog, he didn't want to have anything to do with me, he hated me. He was very violent, he was always beating me. He split up with my mother when I was a year old.

Therapist: So they had you and separated.

Father: Yes, and my father took me with him.

Therapist: So you did something similar in this family. You wanted to have children and then you went away.

Father: My father took me. I never found out what happened to my mother until I was 17 years old.

Therapist: So he was a terrible father to you . . .

Father: Yes, my mother wanted me, but he didn't want her to be able to have me and he treated me like a dog . . .

Therapist: So you think that he did to you what he wanted to do to his wife. He used you to express all his grudges against your mother?

Father: I have had a hard life since I was small.

Therapist: So while trying to be a father you were always paralyzed by your fear of becoming a monster to your children too?

Father: Exactly. I didn't want to treat Jimmy the way my father treated me. I'm depressed, but I don't want to end up that way. I'm depressed, but I haven't completely given up hope. I would really like my son to get close to me again (*leaning forward as if to reduce his distance from Jimmy*).

In this last part a *decompression* movement is carried out. The tension built up before now shifts around and finds a new outlet on a trigenerational level. The conflict initially positioned within the current system between father and son (with the mother in the position of mediator) is moved in a vertical direction and becomes redirected in time to its original referents, with a corresponding movement of the relational triangle. Where there were only areas of conflict and divergence, we discover now elements of similarity and identification and spaces open up for participation in a common experience of suffering.

Again in this case, the triangular structure is the only one that allows interactions to occur and differences to be perceived. Jimmy can discover a different father only to the extent that he succeeds in seeing his father as a son himself, with problems similar to his own. The father can discover a different son only when he succeeds in recognizing himself in his role as son to his own father. However, the possibility of *decentering* the current relationship by the use of a third point of reference is essential. It is exactly this that permits them to explore new ways of relating for the first time, as Jimmy's availability to accept the father's invitation and his closeness seems to indicate.

THE THREAD OF ARIADNE:
THE IDENTIFIED PATIENT AS REGULATOR
OF THE THERAPEUTIC PROCESS

In previous publications (Andolfi et al., 1980, 1983), we emphasized the importance of considering the identified patient as the portal of entry into the family system. We also stressed the meaning of the identified patient as a medium whose disturbance represents an opportunity for forming and developing the therapeutic process.

We would like now to emphasize the therapist-patient understanding and the usefulness of establishing a *complicity* with the patient right from the beginning. The more this complicity is implicit and unspoken, the more useful and reliable it is for therapy.

The therapist can establish this complicity if he succeeds in neutralizing early on the secondary gain that patients derive in compensation for being incapacitated and different. An example of secondary gain is the absolute centrality occupied by the patient at home and often reenacted in the session, so that disproportional attention is given by family members to this person's problems compared to those of the others.

If he wants to neutralize these secondary gains, the therapist must avoid being overwhelmed by the weight of the "pathology," whether it is cognitive, emotional, or social.[1] By avoiding to acknowledge and label behaviors presented and displayed as pathological, the therapist encourages the patient and his family to move to other levels, more complex and less definable. From the level of a psychiatric disorder, one can move, for example, to that of a developmental crisis in the family.

The next step in the construction of a solid therapeutic complicity is for the therapist to elicit the patient's healthy as-

---

[1]This does not mean that we do not consider it important to know how to make a differential diagnosis using various diagnostic frameworks. On the contrary, the capacity to use diverse ways of framing psychopathology is essential in formulating "normalizing" hypotheses.

pects, and not to deal with just his negative identity. If the patient perceives that the therapist is looking for what does *not* show or what is *not* said (often in contrast to the pathological evidence of the facts) and the connections that link it to what does show and what is said, the patient is more likely to collaborate in therapy. This is because the patient discerns the possibility of freeing himself of tensions weighing him down but which actually belong to other family members or other generations.

If the patient's phobias, his rejections, his irrationality, his strangeness, are freed from only pathological connotations, they can then serve as relational markers and lead us to areas of conflict and interpersonal meanings. If faced at the right moment, this process can allow the family to drop its sense of inadequacy and delegation in asking for our help. The objective then is not to deny the symptoms, but simply to move them to another level, giving them a different meaning. From a rigid pattern established by the failure of many members, the same symptoms can be used as markers to outline alternative pathways for an otherwise "frozen" family (Andolfi & Angelo, 1985a).

The signs provided by the patient are a gold mine for the therapist to formulate his first hypotheses about the functioning of the family group and its internal resources. The patient, by varying and modulating his behavior, provides useful information on how to proceed towards the change that is apparently more feared than desired by everyone.

The therapist strengthens his complicity with the patient by giving him the function of a *co-therapist*,[2] who is all the more valuable as he acts from within the family. The patient

---

[2]For this reason, and above all to get the collaboration of the patient, we have found co-therapy with the presence of two therapists in the room not very useful in our model of intervention and teaching. We feel co-therapy deprives us of the active contribution of the patient. At times we have found it useful to replace co-therapy with the presence of two therapists, one of whom has the function of guiding the session from within and the other to supervise it from behind the mirror.

sends signals and the therapist receives them, organizes them and translates them for the group. From the intensity, persistence, or variations in the signals, the therapist is able to calibrate the therapeutic relationship and the timing of his interventions.

Considering the identified patient as regulator of the therapeutic process has freed us from evaluating the progress of therapy only on the basis of symptomatic improvement. An anorexic patient who regains weight or a young psychotic patient who behaves in a more coherent way sends us very interesting and complex messages about the course of therapy and about the family organization at that particular moment. Such messages should not be considered *more* positive than a further weight loss or a relapse of delusional behavior. In reality we are dealing with different signals that require different decoders and hypotheses and strategies appropriate to each. Above all, these signals keep the *tempo* of the therapy, indicating to us when and where to speed up or to slow down. At the same time, we note that the less we preoccupy ourselves with them, the more symptomatic improvements, even the disappearance of symptoms altogether, take place.

In the last few years we have taken into account that the patient, beyond representing the portal of entry into the system, functions as a *guide* of the therapeutic process. The patient becomes sort of Ariadne's thread to orient us in the labyrinth,[3] without running the risk of entering a blind alley or, even worse, of no longer finding our way out.

The fundamental thing that we had to learn was to consider the patient *as Ariadne's thread and not as Ariadne herself*, at

---

[3]The Labyrinth was built by the architect Daedalus as a place of confinement with no escape for a monster called the Minotaur. Theseus, the son of the King of Athens, volunteered to kill the Minotaur. Ariadne, the daughter of Minos, King of Crete, fell in love with Theseus and implored Daedalus to tell her the secret of the Labyrinth to save him. She gave him the clue: he was to fasten a ball of thread at one end to the inside of the door and unwind it as he went on. Theseus boldly entered the Labyrinth and killed the sleeping Minotaur with his fists. He then picked up Ariadne's ball of thread and retraced his steps out of the Labyrinth—Trans.

least at the beginning. Only later in therapy could we be concerned with the patient—Ariadne—as a whole individual with his or her own wants and needs, separating our observations from the functional aspects of the thread that the patient showed us.

The patient's pain and his struggle for autonomy should have been perceived and explicitly defended by us much later in the course of therapy, when we could be assured that they reflected the patient's own wants and needs and served much less as a barometer of family tensions and conflicts—when, that is, individual emotions did not have to be sacrificed in the name of an undifferentiated family affect. In the course of therapy, many dropouts, interruptions, or failures occurred because we preoccupied ourselves *too openly* with the personal distress of the patient, trying to free him of a burden that seemed to us, on the outside, excessive or inappropriate.

Doing this, we ran the risk of exposing interpersonal conflicts too soon, especially those of the parental couple, without having established a good alliance with the patient. If the patient saw his parents threatened and did not trust us sufficiently as therapists, he ended up taking the crisis back onto himself. In this way we ended up "cutting the thread rather than following it," and we found ourselves with a patient who was like a lifeless body, without any vital connections. This protective reaction was triggered in us especially when the identified patient was a child or an adolescent or appeared in some way defenseless.

Substituting for family functions that are lacking or emotionally "adopting" one of the members of the family is a very common risk for the therapist who is unable *to maintain a therapeutic distance.*

SUPPORTING THE INDIVIDUAL
AND HOLDING THE FAMILY

In previous publications (Andolfi et al., 1980, 1983), we have described the need to support one or another member of the family while challenging its functions. We had also said that the therapist, "taking the negative half of the ambivalence which people have toward their function upon himself, [he] carries it to the extreme consequences, forcing each one, once and for all, to plunge into the limitations and suffering which accompany these functions" (Andolfi et al., 1983, p. 64).

Appearances notwithstanding, an effective way of supporting a person is to allow him or her to get in touch with his or her own level of suffering and his or her own fears of inadequacy. In this intervention the essential element, however, is our unconditional trust in the positive resources of the individual. If he succeeds in confronting his own fears and feelings of destructiveness, he is in fact drawing from his own reserves of strength, of vitality, and of self-esteem.

In the past few years we have often found ourselves in lively debates with other family therapists about the concept of *support*. For many therapists support is expressed in the capacity to appreciate and to openly validate the strength, the feeling, and the vitality already present in individual family members and in their relationships (Bloch & La Perriere, 1973; Framo, 1982; Minuchin, 1974; Minuchin & Fishman, 1981). *Positively connoting the positive* is in fact a value in itself and an explicit form of solidarity, which allows us to make contact with the family and, therefore, to be accepted by it. Such moves have often blocked us, interfering with adequately supporting the family in our exploration of more conflictual and muddled areas, almost as if we were no longer permitted to enter the family circle, after having explicitly stressed the positive aspects of the family group.

We were even more dissatisfied, however, with the notion of *positively connoting the negative* (the homeostatic tendency of a system is an example of something negative) as a strategy to stabilize a therapeutic context (Andolfi et al., 1983; Haley, 1977; Selvini Palazzoli et al., 1978a).

In our current work, we prefer to think that our support for each individual in the family is expressed in two ways:

1. Directly and above all on the nonverbal level, by considering each individual as a whole and competent person, beyond what is apparent or the way the family assigns each person his or her part in the session.
2. Indirectly, in the attempt to transform the therapy into a learning context, in which everybody can learn: (a) to recognize links and give complex meanings to things and emotions and therefore to grow; (b) to offer oneself as a therapeutic resource whenever a new problem arises in a later phase of the family's development.

In the past few years, we have developed this concept of transforming therapy into a learning context, along with a better integration of the idea of supporting the individual and the complementary one of holding the whole family in therapy.

In our clinical work we have become aware that one of our essential tasks in therapy is to assure the family of the "solid walls" that mark off within them a "flexible space." This must be done in a way that brings together and dramatizes for each of them not only their present anxieties and fears, anchored to the problems of the identified patient, but also older anxieties and fears. These anxieties and fears derive from other, past relationships and burden current ones and in a certain sense shape those of the future.

Within this therapeutic space, where one can move from one place to another, from one generation to the next, the connecting hinge is always the identified patient. Coming from him and his disturbances, the family can create the opportunity to cope with new crises and to make different choices.

This certainly does not mean that personal suffering or the distress of one or another family member does not interest us. Our objective is to provide a contextual frame that allows us to give individual suffering a different value and meaning. Every time that the family accepts the risk of facing *new inter-*

personal crises and participates actively in a therapeutic project aimed at amplifying and redefining the boundary of the initial problem, the family either achieves a remission of symptoms for which therapy was requested, or a new awareness of knowing how to unblock difficult situations in the future (Soccorsi & Palma, 1982).

Every time the therapist is unable to accept the personal risk of inducing a crisis in the family—that is, when he is not able to be provocative and at the same time to contain the family's anxieties and interpersonal conflicts—the therapy cannot get started or risks being interrupted prematurely.[4]

IN THE LABYRINTH

Let us now see concretely how to develop an alliance with the patient and the holding actions necessary to encourage the family in its search for different relational links.

Sara is a 13-year-old girl in therapy for repetitive and persistent obsessive-compulsive behaviors that have forced the parents to entrust her temporarily to the care of the maternal grandparents. The grandparents, the parents, and Sara's younger sister are the other family members involved in therapy.

At the beginning of the session, the family describes the girl's obsessive-compulsive behavior. In what follows, there is the opportunity to pick out a detail from the whole, in order to place it into a different contextual frame. While speaking of Sara's symptoms, the father mentions the girl's difficulties in grasping objects, as, for example, in the act of taking a glass, accompanying his description with a hesitant and repetitive movement of the hand. The image of the glass and the hands of the father present the first connecting link to solve the family puzzle.

---

[4]Similarly, we do not believe that these criteria can be applied to chronic "institutionalized" psychiatric cases or to situations where the family can no longer choose what to do about its difficulties (as in the treatment often prescribed by schools or the judicial system).

The image just sketched can be enlarged and represented in the therapeutic space, introducing a real glass and a table. Sara's behavior is now in an intermediate territory, where either parent can impersonate her, thus providing multiple images of the same experience. By the way the family members represent Sara's obsessive-compulsive gestures and describe the details, we perceive the powerful tension between the parents.

The operation enacted tests the family's way of looking at things at the same time that the family seems to want to review the characteristics of its own context. The challenge to the system and its theoretical construct is already implicit in the fact that the symptoms are represented by the parents (who have to endure their effects), while the key player, Sara, is obliged to observe herself as represented by her parents and eventually to confirm or qualify their actions.

If, from the difficulty of touching a glass, we move on to *the difficulty of touching one another*, the image leaves the area of symptoms and enters into the area of interpersonal relations. In this continual movement between levels there is an implicit offer of complicity with the girl that can permit or block the progress of the therapeutic sequence. Sara in fact knows that the glass has shifted from being a descriptive link to her symptoms and has become a connection to a higher emotional level.

The first validation of this therapeutic approach occurs a little later in the session, when the therapist gets closer to Sara, who until now has stayed to one side, her eyes half-covered with her hand. He takes her by the hand and leads her to the opposite side of the room to the "old folks" with whom Sara has taken refuge lately. (Later it is revealed that the maternal grandparents have temporarily taken Sara to their home, at their daughter's insistence, due to the parents' inability to handle the girl's problems.)

It is the first physical contact with Sara and the first test of the direction of therapy. If the girl had refused to take the therapist's hand or perhaps had covered her face behind her hands, the signal would have been different. This would have communicated something like, "It's still too early," "I don't trust your intuition and your ability to get into my family's conflict," or "I want to stay in the territory of my symptoms."

Her spontaneous and unexpected acceptance of the therapist's contact confirms his hypothesis that Sara has known for some time how to step into an adult's shoes, moving from the generational space of children to that of grandparents. This leads the therapist to define more openly in the session the area of the elderly where Sara can take refuge and the area of the nuclear family where powerful tensions lie concealed.

By moving from one side to the other, Sara is suddenly distressed to relive her constant shuttling between the two roles (as a teenager and as a mature adult), and breaks down into tears. On the one hand her tears confirm her centrality as a "weak" link in the chain, but on the other hand they *condense* the family's pain. To distract everybody's attention away from Sara, who is now visibly playing the part of the scared child (there is a flurry of tissues from the hands of the grandparents and the mother to the child), the therapist decides at this point to "leave her there for a while" and to move to another generational level.

To do this he decides to change the seating arrangement in the session. He makes Sara's mother move closer to the area of the old folks (Sara is in the middle, between the grandparents), placing her seat in front of the girl and turning to the grandparents: "Can you describe what *that Sara there* (indicating the girl's mother) was like at 13?" They respond promptly, providing important information about the current perceptions of the past relationships between Sara's mother and her parents. The exchange also provides very vivid images about the present relationship between Sara and her mother. More generally, the images allow the therapist to construct more meaningful hypotheses about the dysfunctional patterns of the family.

Between sobs, Sara scrutinizes the actions of the therapist through her fingers, held like vertical blinds across her face.

The therapist is the only one who appears not to be preoccupied with her but with another Sara, from another time and another place. In fact, the therapist intends to go further into Sara's crying in order to distribute the tears around to one and all, so they can reappropriate their own personal suffering and responsibility. If the therapist knows how to grasp the multiple relational meanings of a teenager's tears, he will know how to give her sufficient support and redistribute the family's anguish which has been bearing down on Sara for too long.

It is really the mother, described by her parents as having been a histrionic and impossible adolescent, who offers the key to enter into the hidden and complex hardships of this family. It is she who first takes the risk of taking off her mask in the session, providing important clues for the family and therefore for the therapeutic process. What is more surprising, beyond the content, is the manner in which the mother speaks, as if freeing herself of an enormous burden kept repressed for too long.

Sara was born during the mother's first brief and failed marriage. Her grudge against her husband, described as a vile and egotistical person, was absorbed into the relationship between the mother and Sara as she grew. For several years Sara has been the mother's "adult" partner and the chosen target of all her varied moods. She learned hastily to act as a mature adult, capable of containing her mother's disappointments, rancor, and need for protection.

Mother's second marriage with her present husband is described as more stable and satisfying. In reality, it is the product of the violent, powerful, and unresolved emotions of the first marriage, and is more the result of a practical agreement than an affectionate attachment. The mother's new husband has paid her debts and the fees for the lawyers working on her complex divorce case, and has practically "bought" Sara from the previous marriage. In exchange, the wife has agreed to Sara's conversion to Catholicism. The husband is a fervent Catholic, while she and her family are Jewish who are traditional but not observant. In practice, however, "on account of her disorder," Sara lives more with her grandparents than with her parents.

The case just described takes us into much more ambiguous and intricate territory than the simple treatment of the obsessive-compulsive behavior of a 13-year-old girl. Sara's symptomatic behavior can be seen as an attempt to contain family problems that allows them to be manifested and balanced, albeit in a cryptic manner. The therapeutic intervention creates another external and temporary form of *holding* that permits the therapist to modify the current aspects of the problem and get them back on track.

CHAPTER 4

Playing in Therapy

IF THE THERAPIST ALSO LEARNS TO PLAY

In the "tool-kit"[1] of the relational therapist, play represents perhaps the most articulated, the richest in nuances, the most personal means of engaging the family and the therapist in therapy. It is nonetheless still little used by family therapists, who prefer by far an "adult" model of communicating. Perhaps the discomfort that the therapist encounters in playing is related to his difficulty in moving from understanding emotional situations to representing them in the session. While the need to understand is based on a cognitive analysis of verbal data, ludic representation[2] has an element of make-

---

[1]Both the actions and thoughts of the therapist are part of what Foucault calls a "tool-kit." Is play an action or a thought? Perhaps the answer is that play is an instrument: "The theory to be constructed is not a system but an instrument" (Foucault, 1980, p. 145).—Translator

[2]"Ludic" means having to do with "play," from the Latin, "ludus," meaning play, game, or sport. "Ludic representations"—play, games, "the carnival of life," "the feast of fools"—have become common in descriptions of social behavior. "The game analogy is . . . increasingly popular in contemporary social theory. . . . From Wittgenstein has come the notion of intentional action as 'following a rule'; from Huizinga, of play as the paradigm form of collective life; from von Neumann and Morgenstern, of social behavior as a reciprocative maneuvering towards distributive payoffs" (Geertz, 1983, p. 24).—Translator

believe that allows us to dramatize desires, fears, and painful experiences through words and actions.

Through play we create a psychological frame that "permits one to discriminate between entities which belong to different logical types, that is, between messages composed of emotion-signs and messages composed of simulations of emotion-signs" (Valeri, 1979, p. 814). The imitation of a behavioral sequence in the session—say, for example, a battle—may become confused with what it represents. At the same time, imitation is distinct from the real battle due to the signal "this is a game," which places it, so to speak, "in a frame," indicating that the rules that apply to ludic behavior are different from those that apply to what is not ludic (Bateson, 1972; Valeri, 1979).

A game like arm wrestling or playing with plastic swords activates a physical interaction—for example, between a father and son or between the therapist and a teenager. Playing permits the active expressive of aggression and physical contact that leads to an emotional contact on another level. Through play the possible combinations of ideas, emotions, and sequences of behavior can be experienced and analyzed.

In order to play, in contrast to observing play, it is necessary for the therapist to rediscover first the value of playing for himself and then to suggest it as a vehicle for interacting and searching for resources in therapy. Above all, knowing how to play helps the therapist not to take himself too seriously; that is, for the therapist to consider his own and the family's definitions of reality as temporary and changeable, and to introduce flexibility and uncertainty into his own way of thinking. Bronowski (1973) renamed Heisenberg's Uncertainty Principle "the Principle of Tolerance" to emphasize this flexibility: "All knowledge, all information between human beings can only be exchanged within a play of tolerance" (p. 365). Such cognitive pliability can have a corresponding flexibility in moving from one space to another, on both symbolic and real levels. This requires the therapist to learn to use himself and his own personal characteristics (such as gender, age, gestures, way of laughing or speaking, getting closer or moving away), modulating them according to the needs of the moment.

If he knows how to take on different parts and roles in the session and, above all, if he knows how to move from one generational level to another (playing now the child, now the old sage), family members will be able to move out of the same stereotyped functions and become unblocked[3] (Keith & Whitaker, 1981).

Working with a family, the therapist must be capable of encouraging interactions among the adults and their collaboration in therapy. On the other hand he must consider the child as a person with full rights to show and convey his thoughts and feelings in a personal way, not inferior to the adults. Therefore, the therapist acts as a *translator* of different ways of thinking. Play can become an effective tool for connecting the world of the adults, which is rich in abstract thoughts and words, with the world of children, full of nonverbal expressions and concrete images (Andolfi, 1979).[4] As DiNicola (1986) states, "All therapy is a form of translation—of language, of culture, and of family process" (p. 189). It is precisely through his mediating action as a translator that the therapist can be accepted more readily into the family group, and will

---

[3]We want to introduce some distinctions in the ways families repeat dysfunctional patterns. We use the term "stuck" to mean a temporary problem. We want to use the term "blocked' to describe more chronic and deeper problems. Families can develop a "systematic block"—for example, when a repetitive problem stops therapy. Families can also have a "developmental block"—for example, when the parents get blocked at a certain phase of the family life cycle.

[4]Although many authors, among them Ackerman (1970b), Minuchin (1970), Montalvo & Haley (1973), Keith & Whitaker (1981), Andolfi (1979), and Saccu (1985), have stressed the importance of including children (who are the real barometers of family change) in therapy, it still seems to be more common to exclude them from treatment, especially if the problem is manifested in the parents, or to consider them as miniature adults in the session. "Modern child psychiatry worries about children in family therapy being overlooked and excluded" (Keith & Whitaker, 1981, p. 244).

feel more willing to collaborate actively in the construction of the therapeutic story.

We will illustrate this with a clinical sequence from the first session with the Bruni family. The session is conducted by a student therapist and his supervisor. Marina is a girl of ten who is brought to therapy by her parents, more through the pressure of the teacher than by their own choice. From the telephone conversation before the first session, we learned that the child presents with dyslexia and marked social withdrawal outside the family.

From the beginning of the session, the therapist is confronted with an obstacle, with the girl sitting in a corner of the room, refusing to participate. Moreover, her behavior signals the parents' reluctance to attend the meeting. The therapist feels the family's distress and difficulty in accepting him. On the one hand he tries to include the child in a playful way when the parents refer to her; on the other hand he is looking out for ways to build up the parents' competence so that they do not experience the context as judgmental and disparaging.

After about ten minutes of hard work, the mother talks about the drawings that Marina makes with her at home, displaying a willingness to collaborate and hinting about her artistic bent. The therapist dwells on the drawing to gather information about the family's interpersonal relationships. The first positive response comes from the child. Attracted by the talk about her mother's drawings, Marina approaches the adults with curiosity and sits near her mother.

At this point the supervisor calls the therapist on the intercom and suggests that he start a game in which the adults and the children are to make drawings together. The suggestion is well accepted, even by the girl, who helps the therapist and her parents move a small table into the circle of chairs and gets pencils and paper, creating a space and a context for play.

After a moment of hesitation, rather than starting the game by *being the first* to draw, the therapist offers the father a pencil as if to say, "You start since you've been the least active."

The attempt to get such direct involvement from the father produces the opposite effect. Stating he cannot draw even a simple house, the father is embarrassed and freezes up, as if this request reveals other incompetence. His wife looks at him as if to say, "You're really good for nothing," and in a decisive move sweeps the pencil out of his hand and asks the child to draw. This, however, has changed the context so that the child's drawing becomes more a test of her ability to draw than to play.

This short sequence provides interesting information about the changes in the therapeutic context which took place within a few minutes. From initial reluctance, the family moved towards a tentative cooperation with the suggestion to play a game. The next step required the therapist to be the first to take the risk of showing his own drawing to the others, allowing them to do the same. By encouraging the least active member of the system *without supporting* him sufficiently, the therapist unwittingly reinforced the child's role as the identified patient. In fact, this was contrary to the therapist's intention in introducing the game.

Soon after, the supervisor calls the therapist on the intercom, with the following message. The aim is to make the drawing game more interactive and to free Marina from the position of someone who can relate to others only by being the patient (Andolfi & Menghi, 1982).

Take a sheet of paper and start to draw your little house first, maybe getting the father involved with where you put doors and windows. Only after that, if he is interested in your drawing, invite him to draw his own little house. Basically this is a game and nobody should get graded on it. Maybe if you start with the two of you, who seem to have more trouble drawing, something will also happen with the mother and Marina.

The therapist now faces the challenge to reveal himself in a personal way on two fronts, with the family on one side and the supervisor on the other. His effort to overcome his difficulty is soon rewarded. By offering himself as a model in dealing with his own embarrassment, the therapist encourages the father to do the same. The father begins to draw his own doodles, while his wife and child enjoy watching him. Marina, who has been stuck in the corner from the beginning, moves around frequently to go and see now her father's house, now her mother's drawing (which is clearly more elaborate and creative), and then tries her own, as if to prove that she, too, can draw. In this way the competitive aspect of playing becomes a way to stimulate everyone to find the resources within him- or herself and provide positive reinforcement to each other.

The therapist now confidently continues to draw. At the same time, getting clues from the details of the other drawings, he succeeds in posing questions very casually to everybody about their relationships and their concerns. The doodle game has become a way of joining and at the same time a message about how therapy works.

PLAYING WITH OBJECTS

In both the use of metaphor and the metaphorical object, as perhaps in any form of therapy, we may discover elements of play (Andolfi, 1979; Bateson, 1972; Keith & Whitaker, 1981).

"It is difficult to determine up to what point play is important for each one of us, but it is certain that in the course of our lives each one of us must continually pass through one 'game' or another to reach an equilibrium with the people in our lives and in our relation with reality. . . . We test reality in a paradoxical way through our play, performing 'acts' of reality in a context which, however, denies their reality. The objects we use in our play take on multiple characteristics because they both 'are and are not' what they represent" (Andolfi et al., 1983, p. 109). Based on this premise, we can speak of "tangible objects chosen by the therapist during therapy for their aptness to represent behaviors, relations, interactive processes, or rules of the family in treatment" (Angelo, 1981). These objects allow the therapist to "play" with what he observes, meaning by "play" the creative fantasy that stimulates him to produce new associative links. He offers them to the family, urging them in turn to participate by playing with their own associations.

One can travel on metaphorical levels, transforming words and actions into images, and then come back down to "reality" to find oneself again among concrete and tangible objects. It is exactly this alternation between the concrete and the abstract, between reality and metaphor, that permits the introduction and maintenance of a high level of ambivalence and doubt in the therapeutic system. The "as if" quality of play allows the substitution of dichotomous logic (yes/no, accord/discord) with the more complex and relative logic of *maybe* and of before and after. Introducing uncertainty and probability into the therapeutic system creates a crisis by questioning actions and motivations that have been taken for granted, in the search for alternative meanings.

The more the therapist's behavior is cryptic and unpredictable, the more the family has to make an effort to deal with new questions. If instead the therapist feels the need to explain, to make them understand, he will make the family progressively more passive. They will lose their curiosity to look for further explanations and will remain too static.

Let us take a personal object such as a shoe and see how this object can change shape and meaning depending on its *contextual frame* and the *intensity* with which it becomes attached to different people in the therapeutic scenario. For example, while he talks to the parents during a session about their concerns over their seven-year-old daughter, Laura, the therapist tactfully removes a shoe from the little girl and holds it on his knees. By taking something personal from her, the therapist communicates to Laura that he understands her problems and that he wants to help her. The shoe becomes a relational link when the therapist suddenly hands it to the father to see what the father does with it. Annoyed by this sudden intrusion into his personal space, the father grabs the shoe and automatically throws it on the floor in front of his wife's chair, who quickly picks it up and puts it back on the child's foot. Now we have a vivid vignette about the functioning of the family when faced with the problem of Laura's behavior. With this image the therapist can explore how father's detachment and mother's overinvolvement have become automatic responses. This exploration can be extended in time to include previous generations.

The shoe, then, changes shape and meaning in the course of the session. From an inanimate object it becomes alive first as part of Laura, when the therapist takes it from her, then as a relational link, and later as a tool to open up otherwise hidden conflicts and rejections. The image of the shoe can be taken up again in the course of therapy because it has become a part of the experiential tool-kit of the therapeutic system. The shoe/symptom can be transformed into other shoes, on other feet at different times, and then return to being just the gym shoe of a seven-year-old girl—that is, if everyone is capable of "wearing" his or her own shoes more comfortably.

The therapist's ability to use himself, playing with his own images and associations, allows him to connect with the implicit or explicit emotions of the family. To return to our example, if the therapist paused too long on the child's shoe and examined every detail, it would lose its relational value which grows in metaphorical meanings as the needs and expectations of more people converge on it.

Playing with an object can transform it into many different things if the therapist can appreciate the innumerable services it can perform. It can become a *cotherapist*, which he asks to enter into the family's living space, thus allowing the therapist to maintain a more "external" position as an observer. In other cases he can link himself to the object to establish a better relationship with the family or temporarily to detach himself from it. In the latter case the object plays the part of a "safety fuse," preventing a short circuit.

It is clear that when one takes an object that belongs to the family and transforms it into a relational indicator, its effectiveness improves as the therapist puts more of himself into it. This action, conducted tactfully and confidently, permits him to be accepted into more conflictual areas of the family, where he would not otherwise be welcomed. This *hyperinclusion* of the therapist into the therapeutic system is aimed at establishing intense joining with one of the family members to introduce unbalancing actions that are highly taut and temporary. Just as the therapist is able to insert himself further into the system at one moment, he must be able to detach himself at the next moment.

In still other situations, the therapist can exchange shoes with a member of the family, often the identified patient, to communicate his wish to "step into his or her shoes" and "play his or her part," urging the family member to temporarily step into the therapist's shoes. This sometimes initiates subtle and more complex playing which permits everyone to "step into" each other's reality for a moment.

Imagine that the therapist begins to stare intensely at his shoes, looking thoughtful and perplexed, then interrupts a couple in therapy to say,

> You know, I wasn't listening to you anymore because at a certain point I noticed my shoes and . . . uh . . . I felt very uncomfortable. You see, I don't pay much attention to such things. . . . Yes, in fact they're a bit torn (*he touches his shoes*) . . . here . . . and the heels are really gone . . . I really should get a new pair. I was just wondering how I can help you, because I feel a little embarrassed in front of people who are clearly very conscious of how they dress, attentive to details . . . to style . . . (*both spouses flaunt ostentatious and expensive clothing which contrasts with the poverty of their arguments*) and then I think how different we are, how can I try to understand you with my shoes in this condition?" (Bianciardi & Galliano, 1987, p. 17)

The choice of an object to start to play with, and whether to take it from inside or outside the family, clearly depends on the circumstances, on the "tempo" or pace of the therapeutic process, and on the emotional intensity of the literal meaning associated with the object.

Another way of playing to develop rapport and create intensity is to construct a mirror image of the situation at that moment, especially with rigid families. In these cases the therapist uses himself as an "object." This happened, for example, in a consultation with a Black family consisting of a widowed mother and two young children, aged seven and nine. The children are dressed "in their Sunday best" with ties and flashy jackets, sitting beside each other with their arms crossed, and hostile looks, as if they were defending the family fortress. While the children eye the therapist silently and with increasing hostility, the mother lavishes praise on them to "help them" talk to him about their difficulty in getting along with everybody, especially with her.

Foreseeing a total failure if he tries talking to them or, worse, getting them to talk to him, the therapist leaves the room and soon returns, wearing a more garish jacket and a vividly colored tie. He sits down beside them, arms crossed, in total silence, imitating their hostile looks. The scene is so hilarious and at the same time so uncomfortable that even the mother, unsure of the situation, is obliged to be silent. The silence allows her suffering to leak out behind her mask of words.

The therapist remains in this position for several long moments. When he feels he is really wearing the uncomfortable clothes of the children, the therapist moves towards them and catches their expressions which are now more cheerful. He places a hand gently on each of their mouths and tells them he will ask some questions that are a little tough. But they must answer without words, only nodding yes or no with their heads. At this point, playing with the jacket has allowed him to enter into the most secret fears of this family, in which the prohibition to talk or talking too much are complementary. This prohibition serves to maintain a secure distance which protects them all, mother and children, from the fear of a painful rejection.

In these examples, we saw how the meaning and value of an object can be transformed. If cards are used in therapy, for example, it would not be as useful to play "Three Seven" (an Italian card game) or poker according to the conventional rules. Instead, a different game can be made up with new rules to amplify a specific family's repetitions and relational patterns in therapy.

In this way, we can observe someone's "bluff" and at the same time watch how the others respond with their cards. If the therapist is able to play and also stay on a meta-level (playing to observe, not to win), this strange kind of poker played in the session will reverberate in the daily life of the family. Indirectly, the game throws a different light on the plot of the family's relationships, placing the participants in a situation of growing *embarrassment*[5] by repeating a static game without variations, in which everyone plays a fixed role.

Keith and Whitaker (1981) state that, "When the family comes into therapy, they are like actors in a drama. They have set lines and a single theme. Therapy ought to give them the freedom to change into playwrights so that they have access to their self-actualizing potential. Play is a medium for expanding their reality" (p. 249). But the time it takes to change, to live with multiple levels of meaning, can also be very long and the therapist has to know how to tolerate and appreciate the precariousness of unfinished work.

The emotional impact and the reverberation of what is staged and played in the course of therapy can be incredible. In one case, marital therapy led to considerable symptomatic improvement in the wife, who for many years had given her-

---

[5]*Embarrassment* here conveys a sense of awkwardness, bewilderment, and perplexity. We choose the term *embarrassment* because it grasps the sense of personal fragility and insecurity, and to sweep away any possible confusion with the concept of blame, which provokes and amplifies the individual's defenses.

self disfiguring facial lesions with her fingernails. During the last session, the therapist takes a joker from a beautiful deck of cards and hands it to the woman, telling her that she can return it when she no longer has to use it *in place* of other cards she is missing.

Nothing was heard from the couple for several years, until the therapist meets them casually in a museum in Venice. Naturally, they exchange greetings and comment on the exhibition at the museum. As they are about to leave, the lady says to the therapist, "Doctor, your joker is always in my dresser drawer. I'll return it when I don't need it anymore." The therapist responds to her warmly, "By all means, take good care of it, so that when you return I can play with a full deck of cards again." No one knows if and when the therapist will get his joker, and it is just this uncertainty that makes one feel that the therapeutic process is still alive and productive, well after the therapy sessions end.

If we are able to move away from a reparative model of therapy and transform it into an occasion for personal and family growth, then *therapeutic time has to enter the developmental time of the family and not vice-versa*. Therapy can introduce and leave the important questions with the clients; responding to them may take a long time. We think that there is a time and a place for the posing and working out of meaningful questions left open by therapy; these questions are stimuli that can produce external behavioral and internal cognitive changes over long periods of time. From the follow-up of numerous families years later, we found that the images created in a session and represented by metaphorical objects have a remarkable capacity to persist and reverberate that is clearly superior to those produced by verbal exchanges and interpretations.

An indirect and subjective proof of the persistence of these reverberations is the fact that they remain alive in the therapist. In other words, as long as he perceives the joker missing from his deck of cards as a "presence," the therapist may imagine that it remains an active stimulus in the life of the couple. The selection of the metaphorical object is a creative act by the therapist, who thereby introduces a new "code" to define and interpret what is taking place. The underlying basis for this code is to initiate an unfolding process of redefinition among family members and between the family and the therapist (Angelo, 1981).

Just as the object is a useful instrument to form a relationship and to create a crisis in the family, it is also a very effective way for the therapist to *withdraw from the center* of the therapeutic system. With the use of an object, he is no longer the reference point and the third side of tense new triangles: "The focal point becomes that object, that material element," which is in the middle of the group, "which gets passed from one to the other, weighed and examined, as if it was a deep secret to be decoded" (Andolfi et al., 1983, pp. 103–104). In this sense the object acts as a co-therapist that allows the therapist to stand apart and observe what happens from the outside: "At the same time it provides him with a solid *point of reference* to which he may return at the end of every interactive digression" (Andolfi et al., 1983, p. 104).

Let us try to clarify this with an example. For about a year the Garofalo family has been in therapy. Their only child Giorgia, who is 16 years old, has a serious case of anorexia nervosa. From the first interactions it is evident that there is a considerable cultural gap between the parents, who are both farmers from southern Italy, and the daughter, who poses as the official interpeter of the family. An atmosphere of death and profound depression pervades the group. The girl has been hospitalized many times for serious malnutrition. Although the mother is still relatively young, she seems to have given up her femininity along with her hysterectomy a few years ago. The father, who is older, declares that he has always been "uninterested" in life to the point of wanting to die before anyone in his family in order not to suffer their loss.

All the family battles are instigated by Giorgia's meals. Meanwhile, the attention to food and the pressures it generates seem to be the only living and tangible parts of this otherwise cadaverous family.

Giorgia's weight represents a concrete and simplified image of the family's dramatic dilemma. Below a critical weight Giorgia is a fragile child, needing constant care and attention from her parents. Above a certain weight Giorgia becomes a graceful adolescent, full of life and interests outside the home, and for this reason "lost" to both her parents. Her absence or attendance at school represents for the parents a clear boundary between total possession and loss of their daughter.

All this occurs in the context of a marriage in which the wife was forced to marry both her husband and his family and has always felt like a guest in their house. The husband, who has been pretending to be dead for a long time, has not had the courage needed to define the boundaries of his new family.

In the session we will describe, the mother arrives dressed in black for her father who died after a long illness. Giorgia appears considerably below her critical weight and the discussion is about her weight. There is an obvious complicity between the daughter who cheats, inflating her actual weight, and the father who says that the scale at home is perhaps not well-calibrated, trying to excuse his daughter, and indirectly himself, for his passivity.

Taking advantage of the visible mourning of the mother, the therapist shifts the theme of the session. The discussion begins with the father's feeling of hopelessness and inadequacy, which is now confirmed by Giorgia's symptoms. Father has played dead for a long time in order not to take on new and greater responsibilities. Therefore, the therapist moves the discussion to the life of the family after the death of the father. Father is urged to provide concrete images of the house, of Giorgia, of his wife, and of his parents as he sees them from beyond. A tomb-like silence suddenly descends on the session. For a few seconds the father gives the impression that he is really living his death and is being forced to see his family after his decease.[6] Instead of playing the part of a dead man and delegating the management of his life to others, the father appears alive for the first time just at the moment that he plays dead.

After a few important moments of silence, the therapist leaves the session and returns with a weighing scale. The therapist places it energetically on the father's knees, rests a hand on the father's shoulder, and tells him that the scale and his death are the most important bonds in the family and that he must force himself to feel and to understand the connection. At the end, the therapist prescribes the father to take his daughter's scale and to keep it under his mattress for a whole month until the next meeting, in order to feel it concretely.

In the session the scale becomes a concrete and visible image of the dilemma of separation. This was so feared that it constrained each person to live "glued" to the others in a kind of fusion, without the possibility of relating to one another. They lived according to the rule: "You cannot move apart, you cannot meet." By anticipating the death of one component of this family's rigid shell, the therapist wants to produce holes that will allow the family to experience new relational patterns.

If the girl's critical weight is the main part of the family's dilemma and of her distress, it may be useful to shift the conflict from where the family has placed it (Giorgia's body) through a metaphorical object (the scale) into an intermediate area (the parents' intimate space). There, the parents must confront this embarrassing *object* that makes each of them choose what to do with their lives.

We are often struck by the similarity between our use of metaphorical objects and the implements used by shamans in their healing rituals, when they "extract" sickness from the

---

[6]A month previously, the father presented with such severe renal colic during a session that the therapist had to stop the session and send him to the emergency room of the Rome Polyclinic.

patient, thus transforming it into a concrete image (Andolfi et al., 1983).[7] The metaphoric object offers many levels for changing connections. The clear visual and tactile presence of the object accentuates the contrast between its literal, concrete meaning and its symbolic implications, creating confusion as to which level is relevant to the message received (Andolfi et al., 1983).

Until now we have seen situations where the therapist uses his perceptions to carve out details from the context of the session, identifying objects to use as relational indicators: a shoe, a joker, a jacket, and a scale. The process of creating metaphors starts with the therapist, who involves the whole family. The therapist thus makes a path for their associations, while the family provides the material. The success of such operations appears to be linked to the *intensity* of meaning generated by the metaphoric object. The therapist fosters this intensity by *ritualizing* his actions: for example, acting in a formal manner; using fixed, repetitive gestures; modulating his tone of voice; using particular sounds or absolute silence; or speaking in a special language or dialect. The intensity of meaning is also promoted by the metaphoric object which provides the final synthesis of the *bisociative* frame (Koestler, 1976, 1978).[8]

It is interesting to note when the family masters the capacity to invent metaphor in order to emphasize changes that have occurred or to communicate a readiness to work together. This is also useful for evaluating the course of therapy.

---

[7]One could say that what is specifically a ritual, or at least one of its fundamental aspects, is none other than a particular variation within a family of phenomena, which include playing and the arts as well. The use of therapeutic rituals in the session and of ritualized prescriptions will be discussed more fully in Chapter 6.

[8]"I have coined the term 'bisociation' to make a distinction between the routines of disciplined thinking within a single universe of discourse—on a single plane, as it were—and the creative types of mental activity which always operate on more than one plane" (Koestler, 1978, p. 113). We will deal with these aspects and the term "bisociative" more fully at the end of this chapter.

After a year of hard work, the Neri couple, together with their two sons, Giacomo and Riccardo who are 12 and nine, are drawing conclusions about what has happened in therapy. The couple have been working on their mutual incomprehension and their grudges, which are at least as old as the marriage.

The therapist jokingly announces that today the children will see the changes that have occurred in the parents. He suggests to the parents that they find an entertaining way to present what has happened in their year of couple therapy.

Children: Good, good, start the show!

Mother: (*rummaging among the games in the therapy room, pulls out a puppet*) We can make up a fable and tell the story of this year (*laughter from the children*).

Therapist: Great idea! (*allying himself with the children and with the attitude of somebody who paid for a ticket to see the show*)

Mother: (*inserting her hand into the puppet and looking it over attentively*) A year ago Mama was feeling prettier than she does today . . . Mama was very beautiful a year ago . . . she felt tremendous, expansive . . .

Therapist: And where was Papa?

Father: (*agreeing to join in the fable, takes another puppet for himself*) Papa was in another theater, where he couldn't see that Mama was growing, becoming beautiful . . .

Mother: And while Mama was growing, she tried to find a way to explain it to Papa.

Father: (*with the puppet's face cast down*) I was always like this, I didn't notice. I had so many other problems. Then one fine day, bang! I hit a wall (*shakes the puppet violently*). I got a big headache . . . I came to these doctors who examined me and told me: "We don't have treatments here, there aren't any pills, and no operations either. You must try to understand that this headache might go away or it might get worse." Well, as time went on, I took a little more care of myself and so . . . I started to climb a

little. . . . (*slowly raising the puppet*) See where Mama is? I
started to climb too . . .

Children: Did you get there?

Father: . . . and to face her (*turns the puppet toward the wife*).

Mother: Well, he turned and the mama . . . felt different than
before and she started to climb down. She doesn't feel so
defensive . . . she's become more humble. The mama
went somewhere else. She said a lot of things to herself:
how am I living? How did I get like this? . . . and she
thought about herself a little without forgetting about
Giacomo and Riccardo, because she thought that,
maybe, going somewhere else might be better for them
too. At this point the papa turned around and the mama
started to feel herself being dragged down, but at the
same time she tried hard to hang on. The more she felt
being dragged down, the more she held on. . . . She felt
she was riding a comet. But at a certain point, from the
back of the comet she slipped down to the tail end and
now the tail end is like a grain of sand. . . . Maybe she
will slip away completely, maybe she'll get back on the
comet . . . Mama's still not sure about that.

Father: Then Papa, worrying about what was happening to
Mama, gets close and helps her to get back on the comet.
Once she gets back up there, I'd like to stay there too,
but we need to see if there's room for two on the comet
or if there's only room for Mama.

It is interesting to note how the ludic, almost theatrical aspect of this sequence allows the two spouses to describe the
emotional road they have traveled, both individually and as a
couple, with extremely rich imagery. Without the help of the
puppets, it would have been much more difficult for both of
them to maintain a balance between playing and reality. It is
exactly the psychological framework of play that assumes two
contradictory functions: one signals that what it contains is
fictional, the other makes one forget that it is. This is what

the poet Samuel Taylor Coleridge called "the willing suspension of disbelief."

An important signal of the increase in the flexibility of the family system is provided by the position of the therapist in the development of the theme of the session. For example, the telling of this fable by the couple, with their growing level of uncertainty and precariousness, could not have happened in such a spontaneous and smooth way at the beginning of therapy. Neither would the therapist have been able to remain "outside" of what was happening. The distinct feeling experienced by the therapist of being *at the edge* of the therapeutic story and being able to stay there calmly is precisely what signals the turning point of therapy. The "where" and the "when" of therapy belong more and more to the family and less and less to the therapist, who can then start to dismantle the therapeutic system.

We will review the processes of termination (a concrete term—the actual time of stopping therapy) and separation (an abstract term—the psychological process of ending the relationship) from the therapeutic system in more depth in Chapter 7.

PLAYING WITH WORDS

We have already seen how playing becomes a very complex entity that transcends ludic activity in the narrow sense to become a value in itself, a quality intrinsic to the therapeutic story. We fully agree with Winnicott when he states, "*Psychotherapy is done in the overlap of the two areas, that of the patient and that of the therapist*" (Winnicott, 1971, p. 54, italics in the original). He further emphasizes, "If the patient cannot play, then something needs to be done to enable the patient to become able to play" (Winnicott, 1971, p. 54).

It is a pity that psychoanalysis did not succeed in shifting from children's play to adult play or even better to play *between* them. In a certain sense we come upon this kind of complaint in Winnicott, when he states, "Whatever I say about children playing really applies to adults as well, only the matter is more difficult to describe when the patient's material appears mainly in terms of verbal communication" (Winnicott, 1971, p. 40). If *playing means doing*, that is, constructing relational scenarios, it is not enough only to think about doing or to wish to do. In our opinion, it is necessary to recognize *acting* as a valuable method of inquiry and as a creative expression of each individual's personality in the presence of significant others.

"The searching [for the self] can come only from desultory formless functioning, or perhaps from rudimentary playing, as in a neutral zone" (Winnicott, 1971, p. 64). And it is precisely in this "neutral zone," as Winnicott says, in a territory intermediate between the interior reality of the individual and the shared reality of the world outside individuals, that the "as if" of therapeutic play takes place.

Besides objects, one can play with words—one's own and the words of others—to construct a metaphorical language that originates from images that paint and sometimes camouflage or transform deep moods, denied fears and conflicts, and dysfunctional relational patterns. Such a language, built on visual images, has a much longer and deeper period of permanence and of cognitive resonance than a language based on abstract concepts or on verbal statements in the session.

Even the symptom presented by a patient or a family can become a metaphor of a relational problem, an attempt to reconcile contradictory needs through a symbol capable of reflecting many meanings (Andolfi et al., 1983). It is just through this synthesis between contrasting aspects of reality, in this *crossroad* between situations that may be distant from each other, that the therapist can begin associating and restructuring by "playing" with images (Saccu, 1985).

He can condense the observational data obtained during interactions among members of the therapeutic system into a metaphor. Here, for example, is a unique situation that happened in a case of childhood enuresis. During the initial session with the Schultz family, the father's total inability to cry was revealed, "as if his tears had dried up." Contrasting with the father's dry "bark" was the mother's "thin skin" and the son's repeated attempts to get father to "reach out" and abandon his mask as an upright and somber man. Taking his cue from these suggestions, the therapist introduces the metaphor of *the crying penis*. This unusual and perhaps bizarre image nonetheless gives a precise contextual meaning to the symptom of bedwetting, which compensates for the father's inadequacy. The symptom becomes the alarm bell for the disturbed emotional organization of the family which can thus play with a different hypothesis to review its family structure. It will then be up to the family to provide the material to complete the puzzle to which the therapist has provided the first few pieces.

Then, one can point out a path without following it. In fact after indicating a trail that seems to capture the family's imagination, it can be left there or it can be transformed into something else . . . a river, a hill, or a dam. It will become the task of the family members to *choose* to follow the path, providing specific landmarks, or to *resist*, denying the existence of the path and perhaps preferring to wade across the river or to cross over on a bridge. The family can even resist by making up another track, not indicated at all by the therapist—a beautiful oasis in the desert, for example. In either case, by choosing the path or resisting, the family provides useful information for the therapist to discover how they are responding at that moment to his interventions.

The curiosity sparked by the language of images, kept purposely cryptic and incomplete, helps to tempt the individual and the whole family to participate in a therapeutic story belonging to all.

Here is a family that exemplifies the game of chaining metaphors. John Hiller, who is 20 years old and lives with his parents, has exhibited behavior for the past four years that could be called borderline. This has resulted in a "psychiatric career" with numerous short admissions to the hospital and

equally short and unfinished attempts at individual psychotherapy, so that now John enjoys listing all the psychiatrists
he has "made fools of" in the past few years.

During a family consultation with the Hillers, attended by
his parents, his sister, who is a little older, and his maternal
grandmother, John displays his histrionic behavior. John is
preparing to have fun with the latest therapist on his list besides his relatives, who are divided into two camps—those
who consider him "crazy" and those who see him as a tyrant
"king."

This distinction permits the first move. The therapist gives
John the role of leader (which he is already playing) and asks
him to write on a blackboard who in the family sees him as
"crazy" and who sees him as a "king," since he treats his
own relatives as subjects. John accepts this very willingly.
The idea of being compared to a king appeals to him and he
has fun with it,[9] until he is also asked to give his opinion and
to write it on the blackboard. This is his first moment of real
difficulty, since whatever he decides, he leaves his protective
game and becomes unmasked, just as the ambivalence of the
others, especially the parents, was unmasked when they had
to decide between calling him crazy or calling him a king.
The atmosphere becomes increasingly tense until the mother
unexpectedly offers the first key to move beyond the dichot-
omy "crazy or king."

She states that maybe John is forced to play crazy because
in reality Lucia, his sister, plays the role of a *queen* at home.
Now the father seems to agree with this metaphor, which introduces an element of novelty. In fact the image of a *queen*
seems more fruitful than the last one, especially since it
comes from the family, who start getting ahead of the therapist in providing new metaphors. Now the therapist can
pursue his hypothesis of a queen who dominates over everybody's territory without opposition and forces John to display

---

[9]Moreover, the therapist soon will make him feel even more regal by
placing a toy crown on his head.

his extraordinary behavior in order to keep getting attention and new possessions. This leads to the construction of the first complementarity. Focusing on brother and sister offers a richer outlook than keeping the spotlight on "big" John.

The next step is to test the parents' need to subvert the family hierarchy, which seems to place the *power* in the children's generation and to make the parents' generation the *subjects*. The metaphor of the king and the queen now permits more complex and fearful inquiries, precisely because the "as if" of the game disqualifies any restraint or reproach which would otherwise block open expression. This now allows the therapist to grasp a deeper and more distressing predicament. The problem moves from John's symptoms to the fears of the parents who dread that the emancipation of their children will bring the disintegration of everything, including their marriage.

THE USE OF HUMOR AND
LAUGHTER IN THERAPY

Humor and laughter are fundamental ingredients for playing in therapy. The first assures a kind of subtle continuity, a context marker that guarantees everyone the permission to continue to "play" with problems without feeling belittled or judged by them. The ambivalence of playing "as if" removes the easy temptation to resort to mutual blaming in the therapeutic system, a secret weapon serving potential but useless symmetrical escalations. Humor is, therefore, a regulator of the therapeutic process. If one is capable of plain talk and optimism in facing even serious problems, laughing about them will produce an effect. Seeing problems "from the outside," especially when people seem to be "breathing down your neck," along with laughter can be a powerful instrument for introducing empathy into therapeutic work. At the same time, if humor can grasp any of the more hidden relational rules of the family and move them to other levels, an increase in interpersonal tension will be produced in the session which is an indispensable element to spark a process of change.

We can see an example in the therapy of the Steiner couple, both psychologists. Although their relationship has become very contorted, it is vital for both of them. Their professional practice of marital counseling, often conducted together, has completely invaded their own relationship. Their home life is flooded with details of their cases and the techniques of their work, which they use to maintain a secure distance and to avoid emotional interactions and clashes that they find intolerable. From the beginning of the session the two of them automatically try to absorb even the therapist into this confusion of roles, where there are no boundaries between being a patient and conducting therapy, as if they were totally interchangeable parts. To find a way out of this manipulative game, at a certain point the therapist quickly divides the space in two. On the therapist's side, he invites the two marital counselors to be seated. The three experts now face two empty chairs on the other side representing the marital partners whom they imagine as clients to be seen.

In this way the therapist begins to ally himself to the two marital counselors, establishing a collaborative relationship with them. The more the two counselors are capable of describing as outsiders the problems of the two spouses in trouble, the more fruitful is their collaboration with the therapist. By posing questions, formulating hypotheses and expanding the frame to the families of origin in front of the two empty seats, the therapist helps them become a real flesh-and-blood couple, finally relieved of the burden of having to hide behind their professional façades.

The stress that is created by dividing the field in a way that makes it impossible to invade it from one part or the other is at least as great as the humor of the situation. And each side helps to support the other. We think that through metaphor, the humor and play we have just discussed, join in a process that permits *"combining two hitherto unrelated cognitive matrices in a way that a new level is added to the hierarchy, which contains the previously separate structures as its members"* (Koestler, 1976, p. 644, italics in original). "The creative act," according to Koestler (1976, p. 645), "does not create something out of nothing . . . it combines, reshuffles and relates already existing but hitherto separate ideas, facts, frames of perception, associative contexts." For Koestler, the term *association* simply indicates the process by which one idea leads to another.

Koestler illustrates this by comparing chess and checkers. Chess permits more varied strategies than checkers and a vaster number of choices among moves permitted by the rules. "But there is a limit to them," Koestler points out, and there are hopeless situations in chess when the most subtle strategies won't save you—short of offering your opponent a jumbo-sized Martini. Now in fact there is no rule in chess preventing you from doing that. But making a person drunk while remaining sober oneself is a different sort of game with a different context. Combining the two games is a bisociation" (Koestler, 1976, p. 644).

We have said that humor creates a certain tension in the participants, but when it becomes unbearable the tension breaks out in laughter, which has the function of "discharging" the tension which covers up emotions. Laughter in therapy represents a kind of *sudden burst* of tension: a moment of apparent relaxation of the whole therapeutic system "taking a break." In reality the interruption has the purpose of shifting stress from the interpersonal space, or the area of relationships, to the more undefended and vulnerable internal space of each individual.

It is precisely the suspension of action that follows laughter and produces a void, a very productive moment of silence, which allows reflection and induces everybody to ask themselves new questions. The direction of this cognitive self-inquiry will later be visible in someone's behavior and will be confirmed in the overall emotional atmosphere. Not infrequently, therefore, after roaring with laughter one of the family members, apparently without motive, will break into tears or leave the session or else shoot a desperate look towards another family member or towards the therapist. In other cases laughter produces the opposite effect. From a feeling of boredom and helplessness in the family, laughter can reintroduce a feeling of hope, an emotional shock that reawakens vital energies. These apparently senseless or unexpected affective changes are the more obvious signs of something that is beginning to move, of a vital energy that, if fostered and maintained, can grow and permeate the therapeutic system.

It is obvious that to produce meaningful effects, both humor and laughter have to grasp more general aspects of a family's pain than just the specific emotional components with which each person participates in the affective blocking of the group. We agree with Keith and Whitaker (1981) when they speak of play as an *anesthesia* necessary for proceeding with the intervention. However, we see another attribute in play: that of a *catalyst*, which permits the condensation of tension needed for *a change of perspective* for the people involved.

We prefer to speak of play as a means of *holding the interpersonal anguish* often hidden or implicit when a family is emotionally frozen. This concentrates the anguish and directs it to the behavior of the identified patient. In this way, the patient becomes an indispensable pillar of the whole emotional framework of the family.

The containment of this anguish has, besides support, another implicit and complementary function: *unmasking* the most hidden fears of the family. Nevertheless, if effective and persistent, this action allows a reversal of the habitual tendency of the family to control stress by reducing the flow of information. This *overturns the funnel* and the sudden flood of information enlarges the frame, producing considerable unbalancing. A *therapeutic crisis* is induced which can be effective and productive if the therapist is able to reassure the family that he can hold not only the emerging anxieties but especially those that are still submerged.

From a great amount of *initial compression*, by increasing the load on the patient himself or herself, there will be a maximal *decompression*, with a reversal of the lines of stress. In this decompression, rather than bearing down on the center, the lines of stress are directed externally. This is the "safety fuse" mentioned earlier. In other words, therapeutic play tends to amplify the flow of information and to diversify its direction, permitting the family to return to its developmental path and move ahead.

CHAPTER 5

The Construction of the Family Myth and Its Development in Therapy

THE FORMATION AND ELABORATION OF THE FAMILY MYTH

Many authors (DiNicola, 1985a, 1985b; Falicov, 1983; Falicov & Karrer, 1980; McGoldrick et al., 1982; Scabini, 1985; Seltzer & Seltzer, 1983; Whitaker & Keith, 1981) claim that the healthy family is a subculture formed in the course of many generations through the change of roles and functions over time and across cultures. When these changes are not possible, problems which create pathological relationships may emerge. This is especially true when the assignment of roles and functions is rigid and becomes irreversible or unbalanced, as in the case where a parental function is assigned to the child— that is, when a *family myth* is constructed which contrasts with the biological and cultural world of the family.

What is the difference between myth and reality, or between myth and history? Does a sharp boundary exist which helps us to say what is myth and what is an historical account of real events? One of the characteristics of myth is that it is located in an intermediate area where reality and history mesh with fantasy to create new situations in which the original elements are randomly used and bound together. Myth therefore becomes the antithesis of journalism. Whereas a news report cannot arbitrarily select from among many pieces of information to describe accurately what has occurred, myth grows and develops exactly through its "gaps"—missing or incomplete data—and through explanations based on them. In their place come creative acts of fantasy, which introduce a whole series of questions about the great themes of existence such as life, death, survival, love, fear of the unknown and of loneliness. These are the questions to which myth tries to give an answer.

We can say that in myth, therefore, both the real and the fantastic coexist. Together they contribute to the construction of a working reality for emotional needs—above all, the need to make sense of ambiguous and random events which are more threatening when their purpose is not understandable. Thus, finding a cause that can be attributed to a person or a supernatural being who can be perceived as an enemy or a friend is more reassuring since it provides an answer to something of vital importance. A child's approach, after attempting to determine the origin of some action directed at him, is one of taking stock of who can protect him and who may potentially harm him, by threatening his needs for gratification and dependence.

A child who has developed the capacity to symbolize—using dolls as substitutes for absent parents, for example—is already constructing his or her own personal myths. These are the result of the child's interactions with the myths that the environment has transmitted or is trying to transmit to him or her. Since their construction takes a long time, time is used to reinforce and to select which elements to keep or to reject, according to their recurrence. Individual myths and family myths are therefore closely interconnected and evolve hand in hand.

In any relationship, sooner or later we create a myth, due to the fact that every relationship has a margin of ambiguity. During the process of constructing the bond and getting to know each other, gaps in information are filled by the creation of stereotypes that tend to direct the participants to specific behaviors that serve to maintain the bond. There are, therefore, many things in common between *myths* and *rules*, insofar as rules underlie generalizations and value judgments that cannot be clearly determined. Breaking a rule often has dramatic consequences not only because it violates a given order that was more or less consensually shared, but also because it reveals the nature of the myths upon which mutual relations are based.

This reminds us of the parents of adolescents when they talk with consternation of the "sudden" transformation of their child: "He's changed so much! I don't recognize him anymore, he doesn't seem the same. Before he was so calm and well-mannered, now he's restless, he answers rudely, and has his own ideas about everything." The old habit of "seeing" the child in a certain way, and of attributing thoughts and actions of a certain type to him (and the child's acceptance of this stereotype), creates such a clear image as to push into the background the different aspects of his personality that clash with the usual stereotype. Above all, this transforms a developmental process into a static entity. The myth of the "good child, always a baby" and always dependent, becomes joined with the rule that nothing should change in the way he relates with his parents and, more generally, in the way the system functions.

If we accept that both myths and rules are expressions of structure, we become aware of how a certain rigidity is inherent in both, in the sense that their basic characteristics tend to remain constant. It is analogous to what happens in perception where a perceptual schema is constructed over time, a type of grille which "filters" information and conditions the view of the external world. Myth, like fable, is constructed through a network of events, characters, roles, and symbolic contents bound together and in which organizing elements that have a special importance in outlining a theme stand out.

Regarding fables, Propp (1968) has demonstrated how, beyond the rich variety of individual fables, a great many of them share a recognizable basic structure. A few elements suffice to outline their guiding themes. We maintain that the same can be said for individual and family myths, which are the ones that interest us here. These myths develop in the territory of "the unresolved problems of loss, separation, abandonment, individuation, nourishment and deprivation" (Bagarozzi & Anderson, 1983). The plot follows the "ledger of debits and credits" (Boszormenyi-Nagy & Spark, 1973; see Simon, Stierlin, & Wynne, 1985, p. 209) within and across generations which establishes the appearance and the evolution of the various family roles that are rediscovered. These roles which are common in every family story are based on themes of blame, reparation, the search for perfection, and so on. Symbols and metaphors are the building blocks for the construction of myths (Bagarozzi & Anderson, 1982, 1983). These building blocks grow around a few principle themes that function as organizers of context and of meaning, into which they insert symbolic contents and the personal emotions attached to them.

In Ingmar Bergman's autobiographical film *Fanny and Alexander*, there is a scene which illustrates how the content of a myth is constructed and how this mixes with other perceptions to the point of changing their value as data about the world. In a scene at the beginning of the film, the father of the two children of the title, alerted by screaming at bedtime from the children's room (where they are playing with a magic lantern along with their cousins), suddenly enters their room to restore order. Perceiving the mysterious and magical atmosphere the children have created with the images of the lantern, he promptly enters this mood, taking an old chair in the room. He grasps it with a solemn and mysterious gesture and places it in view on a table, illuminated by a lamp. The rest of the room is in shadows.

Turning to the children: "Oh, yes . . . it's really strange! This is a chair, and yet it's not a chair like all the others. At first sight it seems like a chair for the children's room: it's wooden, a little worn and unpretentious. Anyway . . . its appearance is beguiling. . . . In fact, this is the most precious chair in the world: it belonged to the emperor of China and by a mysterious route it has finally arrived in the room of the Ekdal children. But . . . attention everyone! . . . Come here, come see and open your eyes wide! (*knocks solemnly on the chair*) Look, you can see very well for yourselves . . . the mysterious gleam that emanates from the little chair . . . (*actually the chair reflects the light from the lamp and contrasts with its previous appearance in a dark corner of the room*) Really, it's a phosphorescent chair . . . see how it shines. And now I ask you: Why does this chair shine? Do you know why it glows in the dark? No? Well, I'll tell you, but listen, it's . . . it's a secret! Whoever reveals the solution to the mystery is lost! (*facing the children*) Do you promise not to talk?

(*The children together*) Ye-es, we promise . . .

(*The father whispers*) Ssh . . . quietly, mother might hear us and then the mystery would disappear! As I was saying, it's the most precious chair in the world . . . it was made in China. This chair looks like it's made of diamonds, but it's infinitely more splendid and precious. It was made three thousand years ago by the emperor's jeweler, a great artist, and it was a birthday present for the empress. She was very small . . . not much taller than Fanny, but she was the most beautiful woman in the world. She spent her whole life sitting in this chair; two servants accompanied her wherever she went, always carrying her in this chair. For two thousand years she was seated at rest in her crypt. Her chair gleamed in the

dark and the light shone through the body of the
empress. But then . . . came a band of plunderers.
They broke into the crypt, gave her a push, and the
empress fell down: she dissolved into dust and the
bandits stole this very chair that you see. Now it
belongs to you! The most precious chair in the
world is yours! Cherish it, it's very delicate, it can
break easily. Treat it well! . . . Be careful when you
sit on it . . . talk to it . . . at least twice at day!
Breathe on it! *(The children listen raptly, immersed in a
magical mood.)*

It is clear that at this point an ordinary chair has been
transformed into a completely different and meaningful object of value, acquiring previously unknown qualities. It is
also clear that the relationship between the children and the
chair and between the chair and other objects in their world
has changed. Something mythical has been introduced into
their magical expectations.

Consider situations such as when we seek our ideal partner; when we plan our career; and when we choose one type
of relationship over others. We introduce mythical elements
into people and situations, attributing to them partly imaginary qualities, placing them into the mythical context of our
own personal story.

Family myths and individual myths follow the same
scheme of construction and are closely intertwined. It seems
taken for granted, however, that once formed from the inter-
weaving of various myths of the individuals who are involved
with each other, the family myth tends to be maintained unchanged with the more or less conscious "complicity" of each
of the family members. "The term 'family myth' refers to a
series of well-integrated beliefs shared by all family members,
concerning each other and their mutual positions in the family life, beliefs that go uncontested by everyone involved in
spite of the distortions which may conspicuously imply" (Ferreira, 1963). Family myths therefore rest on emotional factors

based on attributions of meaning. "The myth offers from the world not an image (at least in a reductive sense), but a model of values and prescriptive functions, as it is through this that mechanisms of reading, classification, and interpreting reality are launched. From this point of view myth transmits not so much concrete knowledge as a code that allows one to produce knowledge from observations and interpretations of reality" (Caprettini & Ferraro, 1982, p. 680). Consequently, myth becomes a "matrix of consciousness" (Lemaire, 1984; Lévi-Strauss, 1981), representing an element of union and a cohesive factor for those who believe in its truth. To create a myth, therefore, means to translate a series of real events and behaviors[1] into a narrative[2] accepted by all, in which each individual can discover a key to reading his own daily experience and the meaning of his life, while feeling at the same time that he is participating with the rest of the group. On the other hand, this restates the problem of the role of the individual in the creation and modification of the myth. The individual finds himself within a circular process whereby he experiences the effects of the myth, while trying at the same time to change its characteristics and its implications.

Stierlin (1978), expanding on concepts developed by Boszormenyi-Nagy and Spark (1973), has written of "delegation," interpersonal processes by which the delegated person can more or less knowingly be the carrier of particular family tasks. These tasks may be real or imagined and imply that "the delegated person, usually an adolescent, is both sent forth and yet bound to the family by the long leash of loyalty" (Simon, Stierlin, & Wynne, 1985, p. 83).

---

[1]In our reading, the fact that myth is based at least partly on real elements distinguishes myth from fable.

[2]Narrative constitutes the formal structure in which myth is organized, with both real and fantastic elements introduced by those who construct it over time. The narrative is one of the means through which myth is handed down. In fact, it can also be transmitted implicitly through the assignment of roles, expectations, values attributed to actions, and so on.

Stierlin's work gives us an insight into a kind of *hierarchical organization* of myths in which the individual myth, sometimes without an apparent connection to the family myth, serves to fulfil and to satisfy it. This occurs on two planes—the horizontal plane of relations with the current nuclear family and the vertical plane of relationships with the trigenerational family. For the creation of a myth and the comprehension of its meaning, it proves useful to consider at least three generations. Each individual's expectations of marriage, of children, of work, and of life in general become clearer if we examine not only his or her past experiences, but also his or her parents' expectations, and how these in turn were motivated by the corresponding expectations in the parents' families of origin. If, for example, a father's hope is for his child to choose a particular profession and achieve a prestigious position and the child seeks to adapt to this (or, alternatively, contests this hope), it is necessary to ask not only what request the child is bearing, but also what other parental demand the father responded to in his own family when he first expressed this expectation.

To introduce into descriptions of family myths a historical dimension, as described by various authors (Bagarozzi & Anderson, 1983; Byng-Hall, 1979; Selvini Palazzoli et al., 1978a) and to see individual myths as important in the creation and transformation of the structure and content of the family myth, we must abandon conceiving of the family system as static and mechanistic. The original definition of the family myth by Ferreira (1963) provided a homeostatic description of it consistent with a model of the family as a closed system barely open to change, and subject to forces that allow it to remain unchanging.

It is more useful, instead, to consider myths as structures that are constructed and modified over time. In describing them we must try to be aware that we are facing a problem similar to the one that is posed when we discuss interactional sequences: for this description we need a punctuation that establishes a before and an after, but the process is circular by nature. The original myth acquires sense only in the light of what is happening now and through its intertwining with individual myths of various family members, just as all the family members interact within a narrative which precedes them. In contrast to a historical event, where every element has its own place in an already defined theme, myth comes together through a series of relations in continual evolution. This process constantly changes its meaning and creates new connections or divergences from the original meaning. This is like the difference between playing from sheet music and improvising.

Depending on the outcome, we can distinguish situations in which, despite all the attempts to change them, in the end the situation adapts in great measure to the contents of the family myth; and situations in which, on the contrary, there is a partial change of the contents of the family myth.

MYTH, THE IMPRINT OF
NEEDS, AND THERAPY

In successive generations, myths may reproduce, maintaining unchanged the actual structure and the roles assigned to each person in a fixed way. This guarantees the fulfillment of various functions and a defense of the rules that govern the family system. If the myth had only a homeostatic purpose there would be no possibility of evolution and there would be a stereotyped repetition of the same relational problems. This is not the case, however, because in the course of time there can be modifications of the functions assigned to a family member, with a change in the plot of the myth. This is similar to what happens in every family when it faces key developmental crises and as a result must change the arrangement of its relationships.

In such situations, especially when the next generation has the task of reproducing and confirming the script transmitted, people face the greatest obstacles. At such times, we find people confounded in their search for solutions to problems that are handed down unresolved from one generation to the next.

It is interesting to observe how these problems are triggered by specific events at any moment in the lives of individuals or families, and especially at such critical times of life as births, deaths, weddings, and other life changes. These events trigger "constellations of myths"[3] or interconnected family roles. That is, they activate particular elements or roles of the mythical structure evoked in that specific situation. Which of them will be played out depends on the family story and on the relational needs that have evolved in the family. Decoding the "mandate" or the "delegation" (Simon, Stierlin & Wynne, 1985, p. 83; Stierlin, 1978) assigned to each person is indispensable if one wants to modify the unfolding of the myth by introducing elements that serve as stimuli for change.

We will try to clarify this by returning to the Vianini family (see Chapter 2). Let us focus more closely on the marital couple and how they managed to get into treatment, as well as their family stories.

The request for therapy was motivated by the disturbing behavior of the couple's 11-year-old son, Marco. The parents, who have been married 15 years, complained about his isolation and his lack of interest in school. From the first meeting, however, when they did not bring the child with the excuse of wanting first "to provide a picture of the situation," it was obvious that the main problem concerned the couple. In fact, they did not put much effort into creating a different impression, as if the boy's problem was used to get the chance to talk about their own difficulties.

The wife is a woman of 32, well dressed, very lively and seductive. Her shrill, loud laughter made this otherwise at-

---

[3]By "constellations of myths" we mean a series of family roles that are interconnected in a structured way with many possible combinations.

tractive woman unpleasant. Her laughter sounded more like howling. One sensed a lot of aggression in her, which contrasted with the calm, controlled manner of her husband who is 15 years older and missing an arm as a result of an automobile accident. Their interactions followed a vicious cycle in which the wife criticized her husband, who patiently denied everything she stated. Despite the apparent willingness of both of them to talk about themselves and their marital problems, what was most striking was the uncomfortable sense of distance and emotional coldness between them. From the beginning the son seems to have been assigned the role of mediator between the two of them.

The picture began to get clearer when the discussion moved on to their respective families of origin. Both came from Parma, a city in Northern Italy. When the wife was a child, her family had serious financial problems due to her father's chronic debts which he was never able to meet. For this reason the whole family was forced to leave the city where they lived and had many influential friends, fleeing to Switzerland. There Mrs. Vianini and her only brother, younger than she, found themselves from one day to the next in a totally different environment, with a new culture and a new language, entering an unknown school without friends.

Despite all this, these problems were overcome more quickly for Mrs. Vianini than for her mother who had to put in much more effort to learn a new language. Thanks to a friend, the father succeeded in reestablishing a good position, whereas the mother was not able to adapt to her new environment. In her heart she ardently wished to return home, to be near her parents. This would have remained only a wish if an emotional complication had not occurred. Mrs. Vianini's father developed a close relationship with a friend of hers who was often at their home. She caught him together with her friend and this was the classic straw that broke the camel's back. Mrs. Vianini, who felt doubly betrayed by her father and by her friend, decided to return to Italy and her mother and brother followed her there. Mrs. Vianini's role was defined in the years that followed. For the good of the family,

she and her brother were expected to deal calmly and respon-
sibly with a situation that was "bigger than they were," sacrificing the needs and wants of their age. Similarly, Mrs.
Vianini was expected to make the important decisions in the
family instead of her mother. Her transformation into "the
competent person" of the family was probably determined by
her decision, made for all of them, to return to Italy. She became a focal point and support for her mother and brother,
even after the father made the brother return a few years later
to Switzerland. Mrs. Vianini learned, through this, to sacrifice her own interests and aspirations in order to satisfy other
people. Through her brother she also renewed her relationship with her father, and this relationship intensified after her
marriage, due to the striking sympathy her husband had for
his father-in-law.

The needs imprinted on her by these experiences were
"to support" and "to repair." They became a personal task
through her search for the support that was missing in her
family of origin and her conflicting desire "to repair" the relationship with her absent father, which led her to marry a
handicapped and much older man. At that time, Mr. Vianini
was getting over a series of failed relationships and had left
his last partner "so as not to make her live with a cripple."
When she became his wife, Mrs. Vianini had assimilated her
part so well that she practically became a nurse. Her absorp-
tion into this role allowed her to sweep their sexual problems
under the rug.

Let us stop at this point in the story to make a few observations. The choice of a partner represents a crucial point in
everyone's life because so many things converge on that
choice. The family mandate, which is constructed through a
series of historical events, confronts the individual's expectations to make room for the family's expectations (Bowen,
1978; Cigoli, 1983; Framo, 1982; Haley, 1973; Imber-Black, 1986;
Sager, 1976; Sluzki, 1978; Whitaker, 1982). In fact, during the
whole course of the individual's life in his or her family of

origin, the two needs—personal and familial—have been in constant conflict and the result at any given time is dependent on *the force and the rigidity* with which the family's needs are imposed on those of the individual, and how much tolerance there is for each individual's personal space. This is especially true during childhood and adolescence, when the individual's dependence on the family places him in an unfavorable position for the expression of his aspirations.

It is only at the point of making his choice that the person finds he must take responsibility for his actions and really experience what has been only a fantasy until then, working against the constraints of his environment. This is always an attempt to integrate and to reconcile dissonant elements; to find a compromise that satisfies both the demands of the family mandate and those which are opposed to it in fantasy or in fact (Dare & Pincus, 1983; Dicks, 1967; Nicolò-Corigliano, 1985). When this is realized, the final product is a *condensation* of attempts to respond to these many demands. The process is comparable to what we see at work in the symptom formation, which is the convergence of different needs. The symptom represents the best compromise, seeking to express the needs adequately and to satisfy them.

To return to our case illustration: Mr. Vianini guaranteed his wife financial security and would help her regain the social level she enjoyed before the period of her family "misadventures." Moreover, this man could make her feel fully understood by virtue of being older and more experienced in love.

On account of his handicap, Mrs. Vianini could satisfy the need to support someone who needed her; on account of her husband's age, she could repair the compromised relationship with her beloved father who had betrayed her. Her interactions with this "father" no longer placed her in an undefended position as in the past, but in a position that allowed her to maintain control through her function as a nurse. In fact, the events she feared the most—her betrayal and abandonment—could be mastered by marrying this man who, despite his many past affairs, now finds himself in an inferior position which would make it difficult for him to betray his wife or to leave her. The wife would, therefore, finally be able to have her father all to herself, to reconstruct the relationship which she could not have as a little girl. She had "left" her younger brother in that situation, because "my mother was weaker, more needy of support. My brother is ten years younger than me and so it seemed better for him to stay with my father, since a man would be able to bring him up better. My mother has never been very strong, so, since I was bigger, I thought it better for her to lean on me for a while." At the time, in fact, Mrs. Vianini was 15 years old.

In a certain sense, just as she had taken care of her brother, she now wished that the dialogue that she needed could take place with the help of her husband through their child. But this attempt did not succeed because, "When I needed to talk, even about little problems, once again, there was no dialogue me."

As for Mr. Vianini, we already know part of his story. We have seen his cold and distant relationship with his father, who also remarried, and how this relationship is now reflected in his inability to communicate with his son. This is one of his wife's reproaches—she finds herself once again filling up the void in other people's troubled relationships. The son speaks only to his mother and is very isolated the rest of the time. This sort of communicative impotence freezes into an imprinted need so that in emotional relationships Mr. Vianini's partner always speaks for him. In this need, however, the danger of separation is denied through a continual reaffirmation of the validity of the bond. This "invalidity," which renders him dependent on others, is sanctioned by the real invalidity resulting from his accident that makes his partial dependence inevitable. Mr. Vianini's need to find a mediator capable of providing the "missing communication" finds a counterpart in Mrs. Vianini, who has a complementary expectation.

Appearances notwithstanding, the rules of the Vianini couple's families of origin therefore have many points in common, and similar tasks are assigned to both. The husband's family seems to live in a *myth of unity*, even if within the family there is great distance among its members who are burdened with a constant threat of separation. Mr. Vianini represents, in a certain sense, the conscience of the family, the one who realizes this state of affairs and would like to repair it.

Mrs. Vianini's family seems to have already lived the separation and settled it once and for all, but in fact the daughter feeds the *myth of reparation* and continues to work to maintain some semblance of a relationship between the father and other family members. She goes to Switzerland with her mother to see her brother, and together with her brother she goes to visit their father, while mother waits for them.

WORKING WITH THE
IMPOSSIBILITY OF ASKING

Mr. Vianini has therefore found someone who seeks to fill his gaps and Mrs. Vianini has found other gaps to fill. The two plans fit together. In spite of this, the similarity and, at the same time, the complementarity of needs are insufficient. For needs to be expressed and to be satisfied it is *necessary to ask* (as will be seen in the course of therapy), but it is just this that none of those involved can do. Mr. Vianini's father has never been able to make this request: "I never asked my children for anything. Everybody should be free. If they want to do it, they will do it. If they don't want to do it, they won't. I don't want anybody to feel forced." Mr. Vianini cannot ask his father: "I don't ask my father for anything because he never took an interest in our problems. He was always busy working." Neither can he ask his brothers, whom he never manages to ask to participate in a session. His son, who isolates himself with his tape recorder or his computer, cannot ask. This results in the unexpressed but powerful con-

viction of the futility of their lives. And this is equally true for
Mrs. Vianini.

It is interesting to note how in the family story, the same
reasons for not speaking and for isolation are also powerful
reasons for coming together and identifying with each other.
Parents and children share the same bitter fate and seek the
same ideal. Paradoxically, nobody else understands each
other the way they do. For those involved, therefore, responding to their own wants really means repairing the
wants and needs of others. This is how the family myth is
perpetuated.

It is puzzling to observe that in spite of these shared aspects which make a powerful bond, the people involved insist
on perceiving and referring to their separation and isolation.
It is not by chance, for example, that Mrs. Vianini becomes
very irritated every time the therapist points out her resemblance to her mother. This is so striking that perhaps we can
hypothesize that the core of the problem is represented by the
fact that they have not yet succeeded in separating themselves from each other within their family of origin. In this
context, the more Mrs. Vianini stresses differences without
being aware of similarities, the more she moves away from
the solution to her dilemma.

This then is the first path to follow to construct a therapeutic intervention. The therapist is the one who can and does
ask that risks be taken and that other people in the families of
origin be brought into the session. The more the family members fear an encounter with the extended family, the more
therapeutic it will be. The therapist is also the one who *joins
in order to separate*. Tracing current relationships back to their
origins and allowing bonds of dependence and affinity to
emerge will bring to light the missing plot and identify common threads. Weaving together these common threads will
allow the construction of a new story.

The therapist first of all asks Mrs. Vianini to bring her
mother. Mrs. Vianini initially states that she is not close to

her mother, "because we have such different personalities." When the mother does show up, all the ups and downs of the family emerge, especially the dependency needs denied by both of them. Now that her daughter is married, the mother flaunts "autonomy" just as her daughter has always played the role of an assertive person, taking the initiative for everyone. These images fall apart as the mother talks about the difficulties she had to face and the feelings of impotence and loneliness that have always accompanied her. And when she confesses that she has sought somehow to find a substitute support in her daughter, she reveals a need that has remained hidden until now.

To the growth of intimacy between mother and daughter, there is a parallel intimacy between the spouses. The fact that the husband participates as an observer of what happens between his wife and her mother gives him the chance to know his partner better and to help her solve her problems.

In another session with the couple and Mr. Vianini's father, the latter confirms what his son has said about his disinterest in his children. His loneliness echoes that of his son. A dramatic context is created as neither of the two can ask for a different relationship and they both cautiously avoid hoping for it. The inability to ask has become a common element and not just the patient's attitude.

In a subsequent session with his brothers, Mr. Vianini can finally talk of his own needs. In this case, asking the brothers to come and to share some of the same difficulties can make the wall that divides them more permeable. When meeting with families of origin, as already described by others (Boszormenyi-Nagy & Spark, 1973; Bowen, 1978; Framo, 1976; Williamson, 1981), it is essential for the encounter to end without increasing the hostility or resentment among members of the extended family.

It is often wrongly thought that giving a child the chance to freely express his hidden resentment towards his parents, after having masked it for years, can help to change the relationship, so that the father or the mother can have the chance to "see how things really are" for the first time.[4]

This is only one aspect of the patient's wish, that of making it understood that he is different and autonomous. It is likely, however, that the principal expectation is to search first of all for *a reparation of the relationship*. The therapist must help the patient to reestablish an accepting relationship with the parents. This can be obtained not by raising old grudges and misunderstandings, but by helping the patient work out his relationship with his parents. As Williamson (1981) says,

> This rebalancing of intergenerational dynamics is the sine qua non of psychological adulthood and is the source of *personal authority* in living. The adult generation can offer support without assuming emotional responsibility or burden for the welfare, the happiness, or the survival of the aging parents. (p. 442)

If the relationship is manifested through bitterness, it is necessary for the individuals to reveal their ambivalence. On one hand, they feel hostility on account of their own unmet needs; on the other hand, they make a demand for their needs to be finally recognized and for creating a new relationship. This can be realized only to the degree that they discover in their disappointments—and beyond them—shared experiences, suffering, and doubts. Talking to parents as adults about past events and relationships can in fact remove the dramatic halo through which they were experienced and reduce the resulting emotional distance.

Repairing the delegate's relationship with his or her family of origin therefore means helping the delegate see the under-

---

[4]In practice, this produces a defensive attitude in the parents, who may feel accused and try to justify their actions to the utmost. We have noted that an effective way to avoid such impasses is to consider the parents as *consultants* to the therapist. This is how their presence in the session is welcomed. Their meta-position, supported by the therapist, will open up new relational understanding, beyond the automatic but useless recourse to an exchange of mutual accusations.

lying elements that construct everyone's functions, *revealing affinities* of emotions, of personality, and of values on which the bonds are based. Discovering elements of union is preliminary to any work aimed at separating, because one cannot separate without perceiving the common thread.

This is the direction of our work with the families of origin of the Vianini couple. The discovery of similar experiences between Mrs. Vianini and her mother and between Mr. Vianini and his father and his brothers is an indispensable step for the recognition of their different emotional experiences. They learn that each person's loneliness, anger, and need is different from another's and requires individual solutions. That is what is elaborated during the course of therapy. The changes go hand in hand. Mrs. Vianini abandons her omnipotent function as "nurse" to her parents and her husband, while her mother recognizes that an emotional gap cannot be satisfied through a request to her daughter to fill it up. It becomes even more evident in time, in fact, that her emptiness refers to emotional bonds with people from her personal story that no delegate or substitute can ever replace. To redirect the mother's "gaps" to their original experiences may finally liberate the daughter from her impossible tasks and help her mother restructure their relationship in more realistic terms.

To separate oneself from the experience of one's parents, "taking distance" from them, and to accept that at least part of their story must be different from one's own story is a new insight for Mrs. Vianini. On the other hand, this will permit Mrs. Vianini to see even her own marriage from another perspective, because she will succeed in looking at herself differently, giving up her role as nurse which denies her own fears of abandonment.

A parallel movement takes place for Mr. Vianini. In his case it is overcoming his resistance to ask his brothers to attend a session that contributes to changing his relationships. For the first time a family taboo is broken. The request can be put into words; it is no longer implicit, with a tacit expectation of refusal. For the first time the brothers talk also of the emotional experiences in their family of origin, they attribute meanings to specific behaviors, they clarify Mr. Vianini's experience of "invalidity" predating his accident. This contributes to exploring other aspects of the marriage, throwing light on how Mr. Vianini's handicap has concretely justified his wife's role as a nurse and her unemployment, masking his long-standing emotional insecurities with women.

THE FAMILY MYTH AND FAMILY RITUALS

All that has been said clarifies why the family myth is so important and explains its presence in every family. At this point we may ask: In what way do redundant elements organize the construction of myths? It is useful to hypothesize a close connection between myth and family rituals. We can consider rituals on one hand as the elements that create family myths. On the other hand, rituals can be considered as elements that represent myth, whose function in the interplay between them is maintenance or potential change. Various authors have concerned themselves with family rituals, especially in therapy (Bagarozzi & Anderson, 1983; Byng-Hall, 1979; Pontalti, 1980; Selvini Palazzoli et al., 1974; Wolin & Bennett, 1984). Rituals are a series of acts and behaviors, coded within the family, which are repeated over time and in which part or all of the family members participate. They have the task of transmitting to the participants particular values, attitudes, or ways of behavior in specific situations or emotional experiences attached to them. They lend themselves at the same time, however, to support the meanings that each member attributes to them, becoming enriched in time with new valences and thus providing a structure as context markers for successive transformations of the family myth. An example can be provided from the rituals that are constructed around sick people. The family members of a woman with leukemia exaggerated her illness to the point that she experienced the slightest annoyance as part of her disease. Their careful avoidance of any sound when she was resting became a family ritual. This imposed severe limits on everyone's movements to a ridiculous degree, so that they were walking on tiptoe, turning the key in the lock very slowly, wearing "silent shoes," and so on.

Although the principal task of ritual is to transmit and maintain the family myth, as we can see in the case just mentioned, it can become ambiguous and transmit much more. With the amplification that results from the repetition of the ritual, it may transmit not only the meanings related to the emotional bond and the relationship, but also context markers that render the content of the myth ridiculous and contribute to its change.

Family rituals are influenced by the conventions and values of the cultural environment of the family, for whom they overlap with social rituals (Gluckman, 1962a; Leach, 1968; Smith, 1979; Turner, 1969). However, rituals also carry beliefs within them that are usually unspoken and transmitted in the manner and at the time that the ritual is performed.

Ritual can be both the means to transmit a series of family beliefs and values about particular attitudes and emotions, and the occasion for the individual to introduce into the structure of the ritual his own symbolic elements which simplify the definition of relationships that bind him to others.

In this regard, Bowen's (1978) example is instructive, of a family with small children in which the mother suddenly died of a heart attack. Contrary to what the father and other family members were going to do, Bowen advised that the children be involved in the preparatory rituals for the funeral, giving them each a chance to have some time alone with the father and the deceased in the funeral parlor:

> Some family friends came while the father and children were in the room. The father and children withdrew to the lobby while the friends went into the room. In the lobby, the youngest son found some polished pebbles in a planter. He was the one who found objects to give his mother as "presents." He took a small pebble into the

room and placed it in his mother's hand. The other children also got pebbles and put them into their mother's
hand. They then announced, "We can go now, Daddy."
The father was much relieved at the outcome of the visit.
He said, "A thousand tons were lifted from this family
today." (Bowen, 1978, p. 334)

In circumstances such as the one just described, parents
and spouses usually enact sequences of behavior that reflect
their personal interpretation of what they consider proper attitudes and behavior, both regarding the display or withhold-
ing of one's own feelings and how they should be expressed.
This has a normative value for children. They watch what
happens in order to take stock of its emotional significance
in the people who are close to them, of the way in which
feelings can be shown or hidden and how this will be judged
by others.

In the case of the father in Bowen's example, the fact that
he agreed to expose his children to an intensely emotional
situation, without hiding his own feelings and the pain of
grief, contributed to conveying a norm for behaving, at the
same time stripping away the veil of mystery and uncertainty
that often surround such situations. The creativity of the
youngest child then yielded the possibility of initiating a process of separation from the mother with the introduction of a
symbolic object. This object provided a concrete symbol of the
change in the maternal-child bond.

Besides situations of such great emotional impact and such
widespread social importance, we can think of the rituals created in more common, ordinary situations: for example,
when an argument with a partner brings about a repetitive
series of reparative acts, where each action conveys precise
value judgments.

In a middle-aged couple, the wife was convinced she was
physically unattractive, despite the fact that there was no reason to believe this. Every careless act by her husband was

tendentiously interpreted as a demonstration of the fact that he was not attracted to her, even if he "forced" himself to "act" as if he were. Naturally, her conviction became stronger when, after an argument, there was a period of "coldness" and prolonged silences between them. The husband invariably expressed his attempts at peacemaking with desirous looks at his wife's body while she undressed, followed by his sexual advances. Initially these advances would be rejected with annoyance by the wife, despite the fact that she felt very excited. The husband had to repeat his approach a number of times, almost as an act of submission and dependence, which also served to confirm his physical interest in her, before she would decide to make peace.

We should remember that family rituals have a clear learning function. Ritual is a way to teach family members to understand each other and learn to accommodate to each other, to teach them to perceive weaknesses and to take more appropriate attitudes to achieve their own goals or to satisfy other family members' needs. In this regard, Wolin and Bennett (1984) divide family rituals into family "recurrences," "traditions," and "interactions." It must be stressed, on the other hand, that "the ritual does not appear mainly as a code to transmit already existing messages, but as a mechanism for gathering new information. It is, in the end, an aggregate that is potentially the creator of consciousness" (Valeri, 1981, p. 229). This learning function may produce new awareness in Bowen's case of the children's ritual with the pebbles enacted for the funeral of their mother. We can see it in the case of the middle-aged couple, through the repetition of their ritual. The variations that are introduced, the little nuances, and the different rhythms of their actions provide feedback about the relationship. This is more easily understood if we keep in mind what was said about the subjectivity of perceptual events. Subjectivity here implies that, above all, it is important to understand what meaning each person ascribes to the behavior of others. As a result, the ritual becomes layered with meanings that, leaving aside those that are culturally determined, are expressions of the diverse interpretations that each individual gives to his experience.

This helps us understand better the function of rituals in the creation of the family myth, because the myth becomes an expression of the attempt to give them coherence, to tie them together into a unifying structure, expressing the values in a way that is shared by all. It is in this perspective that we can understand the cohesive function of the family myth in group interactions and the protective meaning that it comes to hold for the family. This also explains why myth is so tenaciously defended and why any attempt to infringe on it is punished or condemned. If a family myth is the product of a philosophy of life and of relationships, with which each member of the family has constructed his own identity, any criticism of the myth is perceived, at least in part, as an attack on each member's identity.

On the other hand, we can understand how every step in the process of individuation must begin with the structure of the myth. The structure of the myth sets for each person the obligatory reference point and the boundary of the encounter whenever a situation requires choices to be made. In the chapters that follow, we will see how all this is pulled together in the therapeutic story and how therapy can construct a privileged context wherein the therapeutic system performs its own rituals in the attempt to propose and to construct new myths.

CHAPTER 6

The Family Drama and Therapeutic Rituals

GETTING THE PATIENT TO ACT OUT THE SYMPTOM

We have stated several times (Andolfi et al., 1983; Andolfi & Angelo, 1985b) that the rigidity of the family system can be evaluated on the basis of the repetition of the interactive patterns that permit each member to play his or her assigned part automatically.

The more the family script is predictable and repetitive, the more the system will be stable and cohesive, at least until the appearance of a new developmental crisis. Such a crisis could correspond with a real event (such as a death, separation, birth, retirement) or, as more often happens, with the concern about the possible occurrence of a feared event.[1]

In both cases, there is a collective effort to maintain the sta tus quo and a growing support of the identified patient, upon

---

[1]In our work with families, we have noticed that anticipatory fears of sickness, death, and separation, which are neither true nor probable, can arouse devastating anxiety and rigid "castling" (a chess move to protect the king behind defense lines), from which the family can be liberated only by facing traumatic events. When a family actually experiences the trauma, its members may reacquire more open interpersonal roles and perceptual capacities of a period of change.

115

whom the lines of tension of the group seem to converge. In this way, a kind of *hyperstability* is achieved, which exposes the fragility while attempting to maintain the rigid structure of the family.

Therefore, the presence of a chronic patient or someone with long-term problems in a family can become very critical to its stability because powerful tensions are agitating beneath a structure that is frozen only on the surface.

The primary therapeutic goal, therefore, is to break the rigidity of interactive patterns that have become stereotyped and consolidated over time in order to reach the hidden and feared levels of interpersonal conflicts in the family. Above all, it is important to take note of the developmental stage that sparks the request for therapy by the family (or by social organizations such as schools or clinics). Sometimes years pass before the family "decides" to ask for help. We find it useful to think that such a "delay" is not due to laziness or lack of interest, but rather to the need to wait for a *critical period* when the family can tolerate an outsider—the therapist—to come into contact with its nerve-center or sore spot, on the condition that he is capable of breaching their defensive walls. Therefore, the "how" of making contact with these vital parts of the family is clearly a complex problem which offers a basic starting point for a therapeutic relationship.

Experience has taught us that openly opposing the family's rigidity is a mistake in approach which is rarely fruitful. In a certain sense we have offered ourselves as "guardians" of the rigidity presented by the system precisely to permit its members to experiment with being more flexible (Andolfi et al., 1983). Instead of breaking the rigidity, it seems more effective to *direct it:* to know it, to adopt the metaphorical language of the family, and then to try to amplify it through dramatization in the session. This allows us to focus both verbal and nonverbal information of particular relevance. To use Erickson's analogy (Haley, 1973), in order to change the course of a river, "*accept* the force of the river and divert it in a new direction" (p. 24), rather than oppose it.

The best strategy for the therapist to make contact with the family and to avoid their potential resistance is for him to take the attitude of "show me." Seeing and altering any of the levels of complexity presented by the family make it easier to construct hypotheses that serve as a first canvas on which to paint images with powerful emotional resonance.

An instructive example of this way of proceeding and the conceptual changes brought about in the last few years is that of the "family lunch session" with families who present with an anorectic member (Rosman, Minuchin, & Liebman, 1975). Until a few years ago we used the family lunch session to help the anorectic to eat, using the context of eating as an occasion to make the situation less dramatic or at least to give the parents back some authority over the negativistic behavior of the patient.

We should add that often we succeeded in our purpose and that at the end of the session we would congratulate ourselves with our colleagues and students behind the mirror, because the anorectic had eaten! Even though this result was impressive on the behavioral level, we actually ended up with a reductive and oversimplified view of the problem. Above all, such results caused us to become agents and witnesses of the patient's behavioral change, separating it from an understanding of the development and growth of the family.

By freeing ourselves from our early enthusiasm for this approach, we have sought to move in opposite directions. Rather than visibly favoring the remission of symptomatic behavior in the session, we have preferred to support it and represent it as the pivot or hub around which all the other characters revolve.

If an anorectic eats only a mouthful of rice at home, instead of getting her to eat a whole plate in the session, we seek to *put ourselves* into that mouthful of rice, even if we have to break it up into so many grains and observe how the patient will eat them one by one, and then connect this way of eating to that of the other family members. It is not the food itself that gives us much information about the drama of such a family. If anything, it is the relationship between the way the anorectic eats and the ways the other members of the family eat that will allow the first shift of levels: from one person's refusal to the interactive net of the family.

Next, the grain of rice has to leave the digestive system of the anorectic and become a sort of metaphorical object that permits an exploration of other areas of rejection or interpersonal violence. The patient on her own represents only a condensation of denied or hidden interpersonal tensions. Dramatizing some ceremonial aspects of the meal in the session, ritualizing the parts that seem most charged with tension, and then changing their meanings introduces an element of newness and a challenge to the stability of the family. Therefore, the family members will find it difficult to refuse to represent what can help us to help them.

INVENTING THE RITUAL

Once we move from the discursive level to a representative one, even apparently tiresome and repetitive parts and roles become vibrant and explosive as if they acquired life by being acted out in the session.

Let us try to imagine the difference between the cheerless statement, "I've become a doormat for my son" and its representation in the session. Talking in images is extremely common in the language of the family. It is up to us to gather these images and transform them into dramatized actions. For example, making the image of a doormat come alive in the session obliges the mother, the son, and other family members to make a creative and lively effort to express the emotional meaning of that statement as well as they can. The sometimes ridiculous or at least comic aspect of some requests (such as bringing a doormat to life) introduces an element of play and of the unexpected which fosters the breakdown of potential resistances and nurtures unusual *curiosity* among the family members, who are more attached to the tedium of fixed and repetitive patterns than to the pleasure of discovering new ways of being.

The doormat becomes a nodal point that increases in relevance as it succeeds in emphasizing interactive patterns of a particular family. While initially addressed to the relationship between mother and son, in the construction of therapeutic story it can be extended to other relationships, at other developmental stages of the family.

"Acting like a doormat" can thus be explored in other dimensions: horizontal (marital) or vertical (in relation to one's own parents). One can even prescribe to the mother to bring into the session a real doormat, choosing one that best corresponds to the feelings she is discussing. If one wants to involve the other side of the complementary pair, one can ask the son to choose and bring to the session the doormat that most resembles mother in the act of being trampled. Or a third party can be involved, such as the father or a sibling, to look for a doormat that best expresses the relationship between the first two. The doormat chosen thus becomes a synonym for the type of relationship.

The prescription of bringing objects into the session is a very effective way to ritualize what is being acted. "The family ritual," state Selvini Palazzoli and associates (1978a), "especially in that it presents itself on the level of action, is closer to the analogic code than to the digital" (p. 96). Thus, to prescribe to a mother to (a) look for the doormat that is most suitable for her relationship with her son and (b) bring it to the session for all to observe together the resemblance, in order to better understand her distress, takes on the character of a ritual that provides a seriousness to an undoubtedly complex and decidedly cryptic action.

It is just the apparent incomprehensibility of a request of this kind, along with its solemn formality, creating ambiguity between reality and fiction, between the concrete and the metaphorical, that pushes the family to act. But we are dealing with an action that poses questions about the meaning of one's own and others' behavior and about everyone's motivation for therapy, as an occasion for change. Therefore, as soon as the doormat shows up in therapy, it is important to invest it with "sacredness," almost like a religious object.

The psychological framework of the ritual act must communicate "that what it includes is a representative action or a 'fiction,' that is to say, an action which is not on the same ontological level [level of being] of what it represents or of that to which it is opposed" (Valeri, 1981, p. 238).

The consistency, color, size, and quality of the doormat are characteristics to be explored carefully in the course of the session, as we also have to observe the different ways each family member has of seeing this new and meaningful object. We can then inquire how everyone uses the doormat in order to understand similarities and differences. Some could walk on it as one does on a Persian rug; others could trample on it with less dignity or refuse to step on it at all.

This series of ritual actions will serve to bring out important meanings and allegories that could confirm the patterns observed or to understand unforeseen aspects of emotional bonds between the members of the family. The principal objective of the ritual, whether in the form of a single prescription or of a dramatization repeated in the sessions, is to visualize the family's mythological system and to foster its development. This explains why visual images of such high emotional content can *engrave* themselves into everyone's mind and have a long period of persistence and reverberation.[2]

To illustrate the therapeutic and lasting power of ritualized actions, we will report a brief segment from a treatment case. At one session, a competent and sensitive university professor, who had been drug-dependent for some time, described himself with contempt, in front of his wife and the therapist, as "a worm." The prescription given him was to bring a worm into the session, because "the resemblance isn't clear." He returned to the session religiously holding between his hands a small glass bottle, in which a little worm wriggled (carefully picked by his wife from their garden at home!). Af-

---

[2]With regard to the termination of therapy, we address the phases of therapy in more depth in Chapter 7.

ter many years, we still have a vivid image of this morally and physically consumed man who, at our request, in total silence, took the longest time to decide how far to place the worm away from himself to express that he felt only like a worm. The "like" expressed by the distance between himself and the worm, so accurately and painstakingly measured, became a *space of hope* for him and his wife. This space permitted him, at the end, to break down into tears. For a few more sessions we invited the worm in its bottle to the session, which we maintain was a very good, if unwilling, cotherapist.

POLAR OPPOSITES IN ACTION

For a long time we have resorted to the prescription as an instrument to promote the remission of symptoms and a possible change of family rules. In previous papers (Andolfi, 1979, 1980; Andolfi & Menghi, 1976, 1977), we provided a detailed classification of prescriptions (restructuring tasks, paradoxical tasks, and metaphorical tasks) to use in various circumstances, with different objectives.

In practice, we felt that this prescribing strategy was an effective way to maintain a clear direction in the session and to make our therapeutic presence felt during the intervals between sessions, especially when the intervals were of some weeks. At times we did this to get a "diligent" response from the family in following the prescriptions; at other times, if we did not trust their commitment to therapy, we did this to challenge them on their own ground—of resistance to change—through paradoxical injunctions, which are well described in the literature (Haley, 1976; Madanes, 1981; Selvini Palazzoli et al., 1978a; Watzlawick, Weakland & Fisch, 1974; Weeks & L'Abate, 1982).

Today our way of prescribing has changed substantially. We would now find it less appropriate to prescribe to the mother (with the doormat) to be more assertive with her son, suggesting openly how to interact with him; or to include the husband in the prescription, pushing him to help his wife use authority with their son. Nor would we automatically resort to a paradoxical injunction—in this case for the mother to persist in her inability to make herself worthy of respect, prescribing a behavior that would make her feel even more like a doormat, with the aim of provoking the opposite reaction. In the same way, we are not particularly satisfied with the fact that an anorectic eats normally in front of us, as prescribed in a family lunch session.

We have moved from the behavioral level and the resolution of the symptom to another level. Both the action in therapy and the interval between sessions are creative means to discover hidden and deep conflicts, of which the identified patient's symptom represents only a reference point. Now we are not so interested in the fact that the mother no longer feels like a doormat or the professor no longer feels like a worm. In fact the opposite interests us—that the mother really feels she is a doormat or the professor, a worm—but in a different way, in the course of therapy. We want the mother's degree of inadequacy or rejection and the professor's self-contempt to become so tangible and well-defined that they grasp and reconnect with these emotions without resorting to the protective mechanisms which block the recovery of self-efficacy and self-esteem.

A more complex understanding can substitute these rigid and stereotyped complementarities: "who acts as a doormat and who walks on it" and "who feels like a total worm and who feels totally perfect." In effect, the doormat and the worm are static images of a relationship that has been described in this way through a series of actions repeated over time. But these images, instead of remaining only personal attributes, can then be considered movable objects, to be used as a "third aspect" of the relationship to be faced. At different times, the relationship can be put into different configurations (both on the horizontal or marital and the vertical or trigenerational planes), always taking on different meanings.

This may permit a reintegration of the contradictory aspects basic to each individual, whose parts may have become split up and divided among the many people who interact with him. In the session, the doormat, the worm, and the grain of rice become concrete images with powerful emotional resonance, around which a sort of symbolic ritual for each particular family is constructed;[3] relationships, feelings, and conflicts can be represented simultaneously, based on ordinary or common objects,[4] barely charged with relational meanings.

At other times we use people themselves in the same way as objects. Their bodies, particular gestures, and movements are used to symbolically re-create moods and emotional relationships in the therapeutic space, through a three-dimensional representation of several levels of relationships among the family members.

We have drawn some of the techniques of family sculpting into our work, in order to visualize and to peg down some particularly dramatic images in the therapeutic space (Andolfi, 1979; Duhl, Kantor, & Duhl, 1973; Papp, Silverstein, & Carter, 1973). In practice, we are not so interested in seeing the whole family, as in "photographing" some details, relational sequences, which we then want to enlarge and to ritualize in the course of therapy.

For example, we can focus and enlarge how the hands of a father and son approach to brush against each other, then draw away in fear at the first physical contact. Or we can visualize the ghost of a dead parent and observe its intense vitality between a couple in crisis. In all these operations, whatever the medium (objects or persons), we seek to create

---

[3]"The invention of a ritual," stated Selvini Palazzoli and associates (1978a), "always requires a great effort from the therapists," insofar as each ritual must "be rigorously specific for each family" (p. 97).

[4]We do not want to discuss the use of the metaphoric object here. We want to dwell more on the object for rituals and prescriptions.

a ritual framework that will promote collective participation and reflection.

The effectiveness of ritual in therapy seems related to the fact that it does not lead to a code that can be learned once and for all, but is a constant stimulus and a potential bearer of new information. It becomes an instrument to give meaning once again to the personal world of the individual, which is often fragmented in the experience of the family. As Valeri (1981) stated, "Because it stimulates protective tendencies and plays with expectations, paradoxes and obscure aspects of experience, the ritual tends to emphasize both what is contradictory or without clear sense in *external* experience (of society and of nature), and what is problematic and obscure in the *internal* experience of the subject" (p. 230).

THE THRONE RITUAL

Lea Grillo is a woman in her fifties, plump but still attractive, tall and ladylike, who has suffered for more than 20 years from depression. For almost half of her life she has been in treatment with an incredible number of neurologists and psychiatrists, trying all kinds of antidepressants and anxiolytics until she became seriously addicted.

This is her first attempt at family therapy, although her husband, Mauro, and her two sons, Giacomo (28 years old, recently married, and out of the house) and Luigi (24 years old), have been fully involved in her drug treatment. Although the motivation for therapy is Lea's depressive state, from the first interactions it is clear that her pharmacological career and her "professional" knowledge about medications and methods of treatment give her the right to present herself as an absolute authority on the subject, in her interactions both with family members and with therapists. Her intrusiveness, in both her spoken and body language, matches perfectly with the resigned attitude of the husband, who stays motionless to one side, with a vacant stare and the manner of somebody who "isn't all there." The sons, tall and imposing, look like two large watchdogs, at the service of their mother.

The first attempts of the therapist to somehow rouse the men of the family have a disastrous effect. Whatever they state (and this is already in itself extremely draining for them) gives Lea the chance to rebut and to straighten everything out. The sequence ends unfailingly with the husband even more absent and the sons "curled up" closer to mother's side. Lea's intrusiveness and the state of subjection enacted by the others are repeated with complementary harmony, without obstacles or pauses. The music is always the same: the "dominant chord" is Lea's illness, which must remain the theme around which family life and interactions revolve. Lea speaks of her suffering, crying from time to time as she remembers her episodes of depression, but more in the tone of a dramatic recital than the real experience of an illness. Her depression seems more like a worn-out dress that Lea has worn for years and that she can no longer take off. In fact, this recital masks the real depression of a woman who is lively and attentive to others but defenseless and unfamiliar to herself. The men of the family have to present themselves as empty people without interactions among themselves, who take on the semblance of an identity only in their roles as nurse-subjects to Lea.

This is the only way in which the family presents itself in the first few sessions of therapy. The therapist feels that opposing the family's rigidity, with the members' well-rehearsed parts, would be an error that could place him quickly on the list of the many impotent professionals encountered by Lea in the past 20 years or so. It would be equally mistaken to conclude the case with a diagnosis of intractability, based more on formal criteria than on any meaningful information about the relational and developmental world of the family. The problem that faces the therapist in this phase is how to construct a therapeutic story that uses the family script, accentuating the parts played by each individual until they become distinct images charged with meaningful emotions.

The Drug Throne (from the Third Session)

*Therapist: (flinging open the door, reenters with a blue velvet arm-
    chair, with a very high back and imposing arms; turning to the
    mother)* We have found a chair worthy of you, a true
    throne. *(to the sons)* Would you two "valets" come and
    take the throne and place it in the center of the room?

Father: (surprised) It's a throne!

Therapist: Yes, it really looks like a throne.

Sons: Is it alright here?

*Therapist: (turning to the mother, who wavers between incredulity
    and annoyance)* Signora, this throne expresses a lot more,
    to me . . .

Mother: (annoyed) And what does it express?

Therapist: Your situation, much more than that rickety little
    chair *(pointing to the chair that Lea has been sitting on till
    then)*.

Mother: Not at all, as far as I'm concerned.

Therapist: I know, Signora, but as soon as you sit on the
    throne, we'll be able to understand. . . . You, also,
    (turning to the sons) take your positions again, here on the
    floor, at the foot of the throne. I don't think you can give
    them up so easily.

Mother: (sitting solemnly on the throne) If you tell me to sit here,
    I'll sit here, but it doesn't feel right *(laughs complacently)*.

Father: And where am I?

Therapist: You, I'm sorry to say, are in a different position,
    more distant, still in the ground, but under it.

Father: Underground? And how am I supposed to get there?

Therapist: You feel like you've been there for at least 20 years,
    it shouldn't be so difficult now to find the right position
    here in the session.

The idea of the throne and its appearance in the session
produce an abrupt break in the course of therapy which is
intended to induce a crisis in the therapeutic system.

The spatial amplification of relationships among the members of the family (Lea in her regal position on the throne, her subjects-sons at her feet, her husband distant and underground), and between them and the therapist (who is on his feet, walking up and down the room), allows the therapist to direct the family script better and to introduce links and questions that transform the meaning attributed until then to each role. By placing Lea on the throne, the therapist communicates to the family that in therapy he is the one who assigns parts. Furthermore, it deprives the patient of the total control that hinders her from getting in touch with her depression and that blocks any direct exchange between father and sons.

In the course of the session the throne becomes a *drug throne* which is always reaching higher. As a result, Lea can be regal only in her condition as a chronic patient. If the drugs were removed from under the throne, she would lose the support that holds her up so royally and so high. If the throne breaks, perhaps she would not even know if she had been born, if she were a daughter, a wife, a mother. Therefore, staying on the throne is her only way of living.

If he reemerged from underground, the husband might notice that he has two partners—*Lea and the throne*—and that perhaps it is difficult now to choose from which of the two to separate. The sons cannot imagine a mother without a throne or their lives away from the throne. Through this construction of links and of meaningful relationships, the therapist forcefully introduces the image of the throne into the Grillos' world of family values. This image becomes a persistent and perturbing stimulus, posing questions for everybody—an image that will be difficult to refuse, because it has become concrete and tangible in the session. It acts like a termite burrowing into everybody's mental circuits.

To give the construction of the throne more intensity it is useful to ritualize at home what is acted out in the session. Lea must let herself be equipped by her three men with a chair-throne at home as well. In this way, when she sits on it she will discover how difficult her position really is.

Papa's Throne (Three Months Later)

The brother and sister of the patient are also participating in this session. The therapist enters the session with a helper who brings the "throne" and places it in the center of the room.

Father: (with satisfaction) This is the throne!

Therapist: You recognize it? (*He then lets Lea sit on the throne, taking her by the hand.*)

Lea: (sitting down) But I don't want to stay here anymore!

Therapist: Yeah, I know!

Lea: And, in spite of that, you're going to make me stay here?

Therapist: As long as in your family's mind your father is still on the throne. . . . You will not be able to step down from this throne easily.

Lea: Then my father was on a throne?

Therapist: . . . of drugs! (*turning to Lea's brother*) Tell me, was your father on a higher or lower throne?

Brother: No, I don't understand this . . .

Therapist: . . . a throne of drugs.

Brother: Yes, I remember that when he had to go to the doctor, we all had to concentrate on him and stop whatever else we were doing . . . what you say is true, though I've never thought of it.

Sister: When he went into hospital he was happy, because they'd take care of him, watch him. The doctors used to say, "We've never seen such a severe hypochondriac."

Therapist: What did he defend his throne from?

Sister: He attracted attention . . . in order to feel appreciated. He always talked about his pains. If you told him that he was well, he would be struck dumb.

Therapist: (solemnly) He was a king on a throne of drugs . . . a king who asks all his subjects to be there, at his feet.

Brother: It's true, it's true. . . . Do you remember, Lea, *the time when he was 35 years old and just getting over an illness, he bought an armchair in which he said he was going to die?*

Therapist: (turning to Lea) So your father decided to die on a throne.

Brother: That's what he thought . . . in order to have everybody's admiration.

Therapist: Certainly, *(turning to the brother and pointing to Lea)* she's very generously trying to bring your father's project to a conclusion. Look at how regal she is! With that string of pearls. . . . She was born to the throne, a queen. If your father would do a painting . . . she looks like a queen from a Flemish painting.

Lea: (her tone of voice transformed) He did a painting of me. A madonna. Dressed as a bride. I was 25 years old.

Therapist: (turning to the sister) Did he only do a painting of Lea or did he paint you too?

Sister: No, no, not me.

Therapist: In fact, I don't really see you up there *(pointing to the throne)* at all. You must be someone who takes things into your own hands . . .

Sister: Yes, that's true.

Therapist: The fact is, you wouldn't want to be on a throne!

Sister: No.

Therapist: I understand you!

Lea: (angrily) But I don't want to be here either!

Therapist: It isn't possible, it seems made to measure for you. *(turning to the sister)* What would your father have needed to come down off his throne?

Sister: Respect from his wife . . . it was a question of respect.

Therapist: But did he respect himself? You have told me that he had talent as a painter . . .

Sister: Him? His upbringing was all based on "home, church, and state" . . . but very repressive.

Lea: (in a more genuine tone of voice) You see, doctor, papa stuttered since he was a child . . . I think he had big problems in his childhood . . . and it bothered me to see mama treating him so badly.

Therapist: I just had a crazy idea: maybe by sitting on papa's chair, for Lea it's a little like being able to stay in his arms . . . *(turning to the brother and sister)* I would like to give you a task, if you want to keep helping me. At the next session, you must bring me papa's armchair.

From the fake throne brought in on many occasions by the therapist, in less than five months of therapy, the family has moved on to Lea's father's armchair. Although it is also filled with medical implications and a foreboding of death, it nevertheless belongs to the family's emotional world. Tracing back her family story, made up of rejections and disrespect as well as magical expectations of acceptance and confirmation, will allow Lea to put her depression into a developmental framework and to give herself and her family members the possibility of touching her. In this way, she will then become more understandable and less of a chronic patient.

Lea sends signals about where she is headed. Her angry determination to stay alive prevails over her wish to hide behind drugs. For the first time she agrees to admit herself to hospital to get detoxified and, more important, to let herself be "guided" by her husband in her treatment program at home. The road to freedom from this monarchy is still long, but at least a path to follow is visible. The throne will be used again in the sessions in the months to come. Lea will be able to *choose* where to sit and the others will also be able to choose where to place themselves.

Staying on the throne or choosing an ordinary chair will now have very different implications, as will whether or not to remain "subjects" at the foot of the throne or "underground." Everyone's habitual responses will be replaced by more awkward but unquestionably more vital movements and attitudes. The family will enter a phase of discoveries.

The need for attention, for example, for so long monopolized by Lea and denied to the others, will be sought by everyone. Even Lea's husband, Mauro, will finally be able to sit on the throne, which he will call the "throne of importance."

Alternating thrones and occupants teaches the family first how to free itself from monarchies and later from the therapist as well as to face life's difficulties on their own.

CHAPTER 7

Periods of Separation

THE PARADOX OF SEPARATION

To speak of separation is to enter a paradox since, as we have already pointed out, we are dealing with a process in which union and separation are interconnected and interdependent. For example, joining with a partner also means separating from someone else on the vertical plane, such as a parent. It may be possible to reconnect afterwards with that parent. These shifts, which are paradoxical at any one point, become comprehensible over *time*.[1]

Director Ingmar Bergman has given us a portrayal of this paradox in his autobiographical film, *Scenes from a Marriage*. Let us examine some segments of the dialogue. The first segment concerns the moment when the couple of the story is

---

[1]Like "storia," the Italian word "tempo" has many layers of meaning and connotative resonances. It means all the things implied by "time" in English, including period, phase, and season. In addition, it means "tempo" in the musical sense of rhythm, timing, or pace. In this chapter, words like "tempo," "time," and "period" have been chosen to convey specific meanings in context, but the reader should also remember the wider resonances.—Translator

about to separate and the wife, Marianne, implores her husband to postpone his decision to leave.

Marianne: Let''s face the catastrophe together, without splitting up! Give me a chance, Johann. This way you're giving me . . . just handing me a *fait accompli* that places me in a . . . in an intolerably ridiculous situation . . . !

Johann: What you are trying to say is: What will all the relatives say? What will your sister say? What will our friends think? (Jesus, just imagine the comments!) How will the children take it? What will the mothers of their schoolfriends say? What will we do about the dinner invitations we've already accepted for September and October? What will you say to Peter and to Caterina? To hell with all that! . . .

This brief flash of dialogue is enough to help us get the drift and the complexity of the elements in play. Beyond the decision to do it, separation implies a profound restructuring of fundamental relationships. First of all, it goes beyond one's relationships with the person directly involved, to one's own family of origin, and to one's most intimate friends, and then to the larger community, which allows the construction of a social identity, based on our bonds. When these bonds are lessened or restructured, one's *social identity* changes as a result. This is why transforming or breaking a bond means dealing with changes that go beyond the act which represents the break. This explains why the decision to separate often reveals *implicit aspects* of the bond, of which we were unaware and which are also closely bound up with our self-image. The type of relationship and its quality conditions not only the way we see ourselves, but also the way others see us and establish their interactions with us.

Breaking a bond may reactivate and emphasize older, unresolved bonds with one's family of origin. The knowledge of this "reunion" with other facets of oneself can come forward even many years after the interruption of a relationship that had served to hide it, as we see in the second passage from the film. It refers to the moment when Johann and Marianne, after having each formed a new family, find themselves like two lovers in a very different relationship. For the first time, it is possible for them to show weakness which had been denied in the previous relationship. This weakness, however, is not any less significant now to the maintenance of their bond. And now, it is also possible for other bonds to their families of origin to appear.

Marianne: (moved) Dear, little Johann, even smaller than you were before . . .

Johann: I've shrunk, you mean . . .

Marianne: No, you are much nicer, now, . . . you're affectionate, tender. Before you had such a tense, anxious expression, you were on guard.

Johann: If you say so . . .

Marianne: People treat you badly?

Johann: I don't really know, when you get right down to it . . . I thought I had stopped defending myself. Someone told me that I've become too soft, too tolerant . . .

Marianne: No-o . . .

Johann: . . . and so I belittle myself, but it's not true. . . . Anyway I think I've . . . found my right place and accepted my limits . . . with the required humility. . . . Therefore *(sighs)* I'm more of a good person . . . and a little more sad . . .

Marianne: And you expected so much from life!

Johann: No, you're wrong about that. It was my family that expected so much from me, not me . . . I would have been content to realize my childhood dreams. To satisfy others I put aside my own aspirations. *(sighs)* You know, as a child I had very modest ideas and I would have been very satisfied with my accomplishments when I grew up. . . .

The nature of the bond cannot be perceived by those involved in it, or they can only see it in a confused way.
"Getting out of it" temporarily is an indispensable condition
for defining it, even if this evokes fears of separation that
pose the problem of when and how to break up. The basic
question (and the fears associated with it) concerns one's capacity to face all the changes linked to the separation and the
accompanying responsibility—the capacity, moreover, to *distance oneself from a part of one's own history and to have less to do
with the people with whom one has constructed it.*

Johann: Do you believe that two people who live together day
    after day can always tell each other the whole truth? Is
    this possible?

Marianne: We didn't succeed . . .

Johann: Do you think it's necessary?

Marianne: You mean, for instance, if we had told each other
    everything? And we wouldn't have had any secrets at all
    from each other?

Johann: But we knew that each of us had our own secrets!

Marianne: In a few words, we lied to each other, and on pur-
    pose. At least I did.

Johann: That's what you say, but not what you think . . .

Marianne: At the beginning of our marriage I was unfaithful
    to you . . .

Johann: (surprised) Oh, really?

Marianne: Low blow?

Johann: I don't know . . . I certainly wasn't expecting it.

Marianne: Oh,   it's   absolutely   unimportant!   I   felt
    oppressed . . . by the marriage, our daughters, family
    obligations, it was all too much. I jumped out of the
    hole . . .

Johann: Bloody misery!

Marianne: If you're interested to know what it did to my con-
    science, you should know it didn't bother me a bit!

Johann: Oh really? Ha, ha . . . *(laughs)* imagine! And if we had always been honest?

Marianne: If in the spring of '55 I had blurted out what I kept inside, the truth would have destroyed our marriage for sure! . . . I would have broken away from our parents, I would have sent the children away somewhere and, as for you, I would have killed you . . . I would really have killed you. . . .

Joining and separating are processes that accompany us through our whole lives. Above all, they concern vertical or generational relationships characterized by dependence, which is reactivated in every successive relationship on the horizontal plane. The original dependence acts as a reference point for successive dependencies and is, in turn, continually redefined by the development of these relationships. From the child's first few months of life in his or her relationship with mother or another caregiver, the moment the child joins with the attachment figure, he or she begins to construct differences from that caregiver. This also occurs through encounters with third parties, and in this way, boundaries are created between the self and others.

Obviously, we are describing situations in which the capacity and the receptiveness to perceive differences are taken for granted. This allows people to receive new information, without which the construction of boundaries is impossible. Under normal conditions, the moment one forms an intimate relationship with someone—when one joins with the other—is the moment in which differences begin to emerge that make the other person different from oneself, and in a certain sense, separates the two.

SPACE AND TIME: PARAMETERS OF CHANGE

Turning to the therapeutic story, we can observe how the process of joining between the family and the therapist begins,

as we have seen, with the first telephone call and all the expectations that accompany it. With the joining, however, also
begins the process of separation, since the therapist does not
passively accede to the demands that are made of him. On
the contrary, he constantly amplifies the frame by seeking to
introduce new variables, redefining statements and trying to
create a new perceptual schema. To explain this better, we can
refer to the paintings of the Surrealists, where the new "reality" of an object is acquired by being placed in a series of
other objects, out of its usual context.

From the network of relationships created in this way, unusual aspects emerge that were unsuspected until then. Both
the family and the therapist, however, proceed cautiously in
this exploration. The initial phase of the construction of an
intimate situation does not permit either side to express their
own expectations and emotions clearly. As therapy proceeds,
this process is manifested more clearly and is amplified, becoming enriched with new meanings. The possibility of asking about intimate details and facing difficult problems
develops along with the intimacy achieved.

The possibility of exploring newer areas and problems allows for the differentiation of aspects that redefine the value
of the elements in play: to construct a new reality, separating
oneself from the old one. In this perspective we can see that
separation is not an event that occurs at a given moment, but
a process that begins with therapy and accompanies it until
the end. Termination simply confirms a series of preceding
acts and transformations that have already occurred.

We can see the repetition of this process, like the succession of acts of breathing, in the dialogue of an initial telephone call reported in Chapter 1 (see pp. 7–11) and also in
segments of the chapters which follow it from different
phases of therapy.

An important transition in this process is the enlargement
of the context which occurs when members of the identified
patient's family of origin are asked to participate in the ses-

sion. The therapist is an active component in the continual movement of joining and separating, which he provokes when he brings together the generations to rediscover commonalities in their personal stories, and then separates them when each recognizes that the gaps of his or her own story cannot be filled by the story of another. We saw an example of this in the Vianini family, during the meeting with the couple's families of origin (see Chapter 5, pp. 105–110).

The therapist himself plays with the process of joining and separating when he tries to move closer to the world of the family, only to separate from it later when he suggests new triangular configurations or by placing himself as an observer. Provocation itself is also considered in this double perspective: as a way of alternately joining and separating the components of the family in the course of therapy.

With Jimmy (see Chapter 3, pp. 46–47) we saw how the initial intervention of the therapist was defined as the compression phase because through it the patient was forced to confront a series of hostile fantasies about his father that had remained unspoken until then, with a resulting increase of tension in the relationship. The initial effect of this is an even greater difficulty in achieving intimacy between father and son. And the closer they get to each other, the more the rising tension tends to pull them apart. It is like pumping the handle of an airpump while holding the nozzle closed.

However, the next movement is in the opposite direction, when the therapist changes the subject to Jimmy's father's past experiences, allowing some common ground to emerge from the present experiences with his son. At the point that the two generations are temporarily separated, redirecting each one to his own story, there is also a greater drawing together. To use the same image as before, it is what happens when you try to pull out the handle of the air pump while holding the nozzle closed. The vacuum created makes it hard to pull the handle out.

Jimmy and his father are repeatedly united and separated

through the inclusion of the third generation. Meanwhile, the therapist joins with and separates from each of them when he asks them to express directly their emotional experiences. He can then detach himself and redirect them to the triangular relationships in which the father and son are involved.

All these interventions create and evoke different contexts. Bateson (1979) maintained that what is learned are certain contexts in which facts and objects are placed, and that the most difficult thing to learn is the *context of contexts*, that is, what permits us to understand various contexts. Our identity is constructed through our experience of different contexts: to these, to the objects and the people in them, we entrust in a certain sense the "memory" of our story. These contexts provide important mediators and support for the expression of feelings and give us continuity through successive relationships.

Viewing a scene of nature together with a person whom one cares about or using an object during a meaningful relationship are events that partly shape experience; repeating them can allow one to rediscover emotional experiences that are reevoked. They serve, that is, to make specific emotions and relationships concrete and tangible. Even the memories of emotions and feelings apparently unattached to specific objects and persons are possible only in so far as they are connected to a particular context that supports it. Each context is an ensemble of all the elements described above. In a certain sense the loss of any of its meaningful elements is a kind of separation. For this reason, moving away from his place of origin is sometimes quite traumatic for a child, in spite of his parents' being present, and the desire to return to one's origins is powerful even in many adults.

On the other hand, the contexts that follow each other over a lifetime always seem to be "separate" from one another. Only in mental illness can one live with the illusion of stopping time and keeping together experiences that are separated by time. The problem is, therefore, how to maintain continuity, in spite of differences and losses. Besides the denial of reality as a solution to this dilemma, the other possibility is to construct a context in which to unify the diverse experiences of separation.

Therefore, the principal task of the therapist who sets out to reconstruct is to discover *elements of mediation* that "stitch together" contradictory situations. From this point of view, then, the therapist is the medium for connecting different contexts and experiences. The therapeutic space thus becomes the meeting point of different contexts from different times and the place for the construction of a context of contexts. The therapeutic relationship and the people who participate in it make up the support material to which new experiences are "anchored" and join to become part of each individual's story.

In this perspective, the encounters with Mrs. Vianini's mother and Mr. Vianini's brothers connect the past contexts and the present one through the presence of the therapist (see Chapter 5). What seemed obvious to the wife at the beginning of therapy—that her husband did not ask anything about her past life and her relationships with her family of origin—is not obvious now, two years later. This happens when the wife ceases to belong to her family of origin (and becomes aware of it) and consequently feels the lack of a marriage bond, which was missing from the beginning. At this point, she asks her husband dramatically, "How is it possible that in 20 years of marriage you've never asked me anything about my relationship with my parents, about my family, about my past life?" Because of the process of therapy, even after many years, new questions open up, new separations are now recognized, and new unions are sought.

Similarly, in the case of Jimmy and his father (Chapter 3), the therapist's recalling of the father's relationship with his family of origin, and therefore of an image of him as a child with his parents, creates new contact with his son by a realignment of time and of contexts. It is precisely this continual uniting and separating of contexts from different times—this entering and leaving of the same therapist into different periods of each person's life—that contributes to creating a new sense of time and the plot of a new story.

The "tempo" of encounters follows the rhythm of the therapeutic relationship and its natural evolution. It is important to find a balance between the needs of "holding" the family against the disruptive force of its problems and the need to avoid making such a demanding intervention that it translates into a reinforcement of their inertia. The family's inertia will lead the members to maintain that "nothing has changed," simply because there has not been enough time to experience the change. For this reason, we maintain that an interval between sessions of two-to-four weeks is necessary to reflect the latency period of new experiences in family life.

If the intervals between sessions are the time needed by the family and by the therapeutic system to elaborate the stimuli introduced and to produce elements of novelty (Selvini Palazzoli, 1980), their duration also reflects the different phases of therapy. In the early phase of the therapeutic system, the formation of alliance necessary for its good functioning requires shorter intervals between sessions. Later in the process of therapy, the family "shows its readiness to test its autonomy independent of the support of the therapist, and the therapeutic process moves toward a gradual resolution" (Andolfi et al., 1983, p. 82). If the therapist feels that this readiness corresponds to a need to transform the family, to its search for different experiences and new solutions, he "may openly side with the family's changes and reassure the family about their accomplishments" (Andolfi et al., 1983, p. 82). His support is often important to avoid the temptation of returning to the previous situation, under the pressure of the existential difficulties and the fear of the unknown that every transitional phase brings.

Therefore, the frequency of meetings will diminish. As we stated in Chapter 4, to shift from a reparative model of therapy and transform it into an occasion for personal and group growth, therapeutic time must enter the developmental time of the group, and not the other way around. Therapy will be able to introduce and leave important questions with the clients. Responding to these questions may also take a long time. We think that there is a time and a place for posing and working out meaningful questions left open by therapy; these questions are stimuli that can produce external behavioral and internal cognitive changes over long periods of time.

From this point of view, we no longer see the disappearance of the symptom in the patient as the only key element to be resolved. We consider therapy successful when:

1. the identified patient's behavior appears profoundly modified, and the symptoms for which therapy was requested have disappeared or, at least, have decreased in intensity;
2. the family has reset its developmental tempo and the identified patient no longer has the function of stopping it by placing himself in the center of family conflicts. Anyone can speak openly about other relationships and important unresolved problems between different parts of the family, without the patient anticipating and automatically being involved in every interaction.

The second outcome is even more important than the first because we have often observed considerable changes in the identified patient, without necessarily seeing changes in the way the other family members related among themselves. This difficulty in finding a developmental period and a generational space suitable to deal with family problems has frequently made the patient relapse into his role as a reassuring "pillar" for the family. The function of family "savior" may also be forced onto other members, to the detriment of their space for growth.

These experiences have given us the opportunity to evaluate the success of therapy more on the basis of the overall development of the family than on the improvement of the

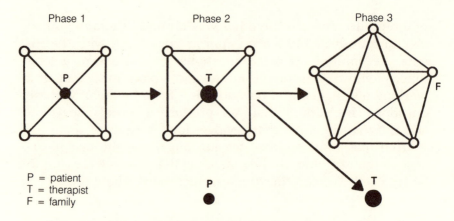

Figure 7.1. New Schema of the Progression of the Therapeutic Process.

symptom alone. Nonetheless, this does not mean that the symptom is neglected.

This conclusion has led us to modify the schema we used in our last book (Andolfi et al., 1983, Fig. 5, p. 83) to represent the progression of the therapeutic process. The new schema is indicated in Figure 7.1.

The diagram divides the therapeutic process into three main phases. In the first, the identified patient is present in every relational triangle. He becomes rapidly involved (and in turn actively involves someone else) in every interaction between two members of the family. In the second phase, the therapist voluntarily substitutes himself for the patient in this function, acting as a third party in various triangular configurations, while the patient is placed in an external position as an observer. In the third phase, corresponding with the end of therapy, the therapist separates himself from the group, and the interactive triangles form much more freely because he is no longer the main person who is involved in the various triangles. Naturally, this schema refers to an ideal situation, since we all know very well that no family changes its relational schemata completely, but only makes them more elastic or modifies them partially.

FOLLOW-UP

The long-term evaluation of therapy is unquestionably a complex procedure, often incomplete or disregarded altogether. Our concept is that to do a follow-up study we should use the same criteria that guided our cognitive operations in the course of therapy.

If, as we have stated, we do not see therapy as reparative, aimed simply at the resolution of the symptom, but as representing the attempt to modify the meanings attributed to problematic situations, in the follow-up we must examine them. That is, we must see to what degree the relational meaning of the symptom and of the family's reaction to it has changed. If the symptoms have disappeared, we must observe how the relational configurations of the family and each person's personal space (including the patient's) has been modified.

If the objective of therapy is to reactivate the family's developmental period—an operation we call the "normalization" of the pathological situation—we must observe to what degree the family has succeeded in regaining a historical perspective. Such a perspective allows the family to live in the present, without experiencing it as a repetition of the past or as a compulsory blueprint for the future. A more fluid sense of time will have a corresponding recovery of more well-defined generational spaces in order to face new and inevitable developmental problems.

With this notion, we can pose different questions: for example, how to evaluate the reacquired intimacy of a couple or the acceptance of a conflictual relationship with a parent, or the shift from destructive interactions to a process of growing consensus.

Currently, we are more interested at long-term follow-up in evaluating the capacity of the family to reorganize than with the behavior of one of its members. Symptoms and their development serve as reference points to frame the entire learning process of the family. If the family has regained faith in its own resources and has used them concretely, overcoming the impasse that brought the family into therapy, then the impasse will be used productively and, through its integration with new elements, is transformed into an opportunity for growth. The family thus becomes a potential *relational laboratory* where different relationships, functions, and ways of being are experienced.

When someone in the family says that the patient "has really changed" or that another member is "different now," in reality he or she is talking about complex changes and reciprocities in which both the observer who sees a different reality and what is presented as different have changed. It is the circularity of the experience of change that allows us to appraise it and support it over time. We can also make further corrections and adjustments in this constantly changing context, where each person feels he is participating in a shifting reality which is more unpredictable and less "mythicized."

If the first question that is posed is *how* to interpret the changes, the second is *when* to see the family again for a follow-up interview. That is, how long after the end of therapy is it useful to meet the family again or, at least, to gather information from them on the telephone?

In fact, the interval between the end of our sessions and our follow-up has become progressively longer and is now a period of two to three years. We will try to explain the reasons for this, starting with the way in which we generally conclude therapy.

The termination of therapy does not occur in an abrupt and final way. As we have emphasized, we are dealing with a process of separation which takes place over a long time, with a progressive lengthening of the intervals between the sessions, so that one could almost say the final session is already a first follow-up.

Let us take the example of a two-year course of therapy. In the first year and a half we would probably meet every two or three weeks, while in the last six months the sessions would be further apart, with intervals of two or three months. It is also possible that at the end of two years of therapy we would set an appointment for six to eight months later, often anchoring it to some foreseeable family developmental event. Examples are: the birth of a child, the end of the school year, the return of a student from studying elsewhere, a couple's change of residence, the end of a long hospital stay, or one of the children leaving home.

In other cases, the first follow-up meeting after a few months can be planned to consolidate the changes that have already occurred in the course of therapy. For example, with a couple who have undergone a serious marital crisis and have rediscovered through therapy a more mature and deeply felt intimacy, the therapist can make an appointment that signals the point at which the two spouses will have decided to "remarry." Then our meeting will serve to evaluate the two partners after a kind of second honeymoon. This therapeutic ritual (having the couple "marry again") may foster a further definition of the relationship, first of all between themselves, and then with the therapist, who will present himself as a witness of their new bond.

In other cases, the date of the meeting can be left open. For example, the therapist can say that he is willing to conduct a follow-up interview only when a grandchild is born. Doing this implicitly encourages a generational shift that allows the parents to experience being grandparents and allows the children to "graduate" as children and take on the responsibility of parents. This is especially indicated when there has been a lot of work in therapy on a "frozen" period, where the family seems to be stuck at the children's generation and worried about letting go of the security of prolonged dependence. Or else, when mourning has frozen both objects and people for years from the moment of their loss, we can say that we are ready to see the family again "when the shrine has become desecrated and the house is restored."

Proceeding in this fashion, follow-up can be understood as a subtle continuation of therapy in which the intervals between meetings have gradually lengthened, becoming themselves therapeutic spaces. If, for a long time, the therapist has been a mediator and/or a director of the therapeutic story,

now the family really becomes the *protagonist* of the therapy
and *home* becomes the place for developing and testing what
the family members have learned in the therapist's office. Although he remains meaningful, the therapist now goes to the
sidelines in order to allow the questions and the images constructed together in the course of therapy to plant their seeds
and to bear fruit in the family.

From long-term follow-up[2] conducted with many families,
we have found that the images created in a session and represented by metaphoric objects or dramatized actions have a
remarkable capacity to persist and reverberate that is clearly
superior to those produced by verbal interchanges.

We have become more and more convinced that each individual has a place for mental storage and a time for the elaboration of meaningful stimuli introduced by therapy. Such
stimuli can produce external changes in individuals, both on
the behavioral and physical levels, that will bring an emotional reorganization of the whole family. A suffocating and
disparaging mother may arrive a few years later looking vital
and assertive, while her adolescent son who was very with-
drawn appears more free and more expressive even in his
movements. All this may correspond to a recovery of a sense
of humor and a playful attitude in the father, previously
viewed as a pedantic, old-fashioned man. Variations in relationships and interpersonal functions may also be reflected in
environmental changes. The choice of new furniture and new
furnishings, painting the walls, changing apartments or moving, new work activities, and the entry of a pet into the
household may all be expressions of a recovered vitality in
the family.

If we then examine these changes in more depth, we become aware that the most meaningful changes occur at the
cognitive level. The mental image of self and others has been

---

[2]We are currently conducting a more systematic study of the outcome of
100 cases of family therapy, in order to evaluate the results of therapy in
relation to the type of symptoms presented by the family.

slowly modified, producing important transformations in the family's values.

Another way to keep therapy active after the termination of the sessions is to give the family objects charged with metaphorical meanings and emotional implications both for the patient and for his family. In successive follow-up interviews, we can observe the changes that have occurred and the questions that are still unresolved. We saw in Chapter 4, for example, how a joker still had the power to evoke vivid images several years after the final session of marital therapy. The therapist, as you will remember, had given it to the patient (a middle-aged woman who for many years had given herself disfiguring facial lesions) at the last therapy session, adding that she could return it when she no longer needed to use it "in the place" of other missing cards.

The woman, encountering the therapist by chance in a museum in Venice, approached him and said, "Doctor, your joker is always in my dresser drawer. I'll return it when I don't need it anymore." The therapist responded to her warmly, "By all means, take good care of it, so that when you return it I'll be able to play with a full deck of cards again." The joker symbolized a commitment to change that accompanied the couple in their development. At the same time it was a tangible sign of their uncertainty about the future that kept alive and productive what was mobilized in the course of therapy, even after a considerable period of time.

We have a letter from an anorectic patient, Carla, that was sent to the therapist three years after the last session of therapy. It is a good example to evaluate whether the identified patient has stopped functioning as a pillar of the family and become a freer adolescent, with the expected conflicts of her age and the cultural context she lives in.

In order to understand the text of the letter it is necessary to go back to the final session, when the therapist gave Carla, then 15, a "crazy ball" (a ball with a bag of sand inside it so that when you throw it, its path is unpredictable). During the course of therapy, all the family members were activated by the crazy ball and its likeness to Carla.[3] Because of the considerable emotional value this object assumed in the sessions as a stimulus, the therapist gave it to Carla. He recommended that she keep it in her room in open view and that she not return it as long as the family needed the crazy ball.

Here is the letter:

> I'm finally returning your crazy ball.
>
> I'm sorry to have kept it so long—a little out of laziness, a little for fear of meeting you again after almost three years.
>
> Anyway, I think that you really want it back and so I'll leave it here for you [with the therapist's secretary]. I'm going through a strange time, I don't know what's happening to me. I'm not alone anymore like I used to be, but I feel sad. I like what I'm doing (I play classical guitar and I'm taking acting lessons) and I'm also interested in some of my high school subjects. I really have a lot of things to do and I can say I'm satisfied. I have lots of hope and I'm trying to improve my relationships with other people. I've even learned to be more sociable and to play the clown a little.
>
> I don't even know if I'm me or not anymore. I only know that I used to be different. But maybe one should never look back, but always look straight ahead.
>
> Sometimes I'd still like to be an anorectic, sometimes I think I was never sick, and sometimes, on the contrary, I think I didn't get any better.
>
> I don't know if you remember what you told me. One time you told me that I was already dead inside. I cried then, but now I think that you were right, even if I sincerely hope to come back to life one day. You also told me that inside I was sort of like Don Quixote. But this phrase continues to puzzle me. And if on one hand I want to be a Don Quixote all my life, on the other hand I

---

[3]For further details of Carla's case, see Chapter 6, "Metaphor and the Metaphoric Object in Therapy" in our book (Andolfi et al., 1983, pp. 94–97, 104–107).

ask myself if it isn't better for everybody's sake to have a few more Sancho Panzas and a few less Don Quixotes.

I don't know when we'll see each other again. Anyway, thanks for not forgetting about me.

Carla

One could make many comments about the contents of this letter. We will limit ourselves to some considerations that are useful for the analysis of the follow-up. First of all, Carla's letter confirms what we have stated repeatedly in this book: that the therapeutic process remains active and at work even at a distance, after the meetings have ended.

On a certain level, we have become convinced that *therapy begins at the moment it ends*. In other words, the most fertile and productive period for incorporating a process of change in the family begins with the family's detachment and their separation from the therapist.

Physical detachment fosters the continuation of the therapeutic relationship at a more abstract and mediated level. If the therapist has been an important connection in the reconstruction of the family story, he remains present and active. He will thus be incorporated in those images and in those objects that have produced a great emotional impact on the group. The therapist is concretely present in the crazy ball and in the meaningful relationships attributed to it during the course of therapy. At the same time, he is and must remain unconnected with the family's and Carla's subsequent elaboration of what has been enacted and recreated in the session.

Moreover, a curiosity about herself and the outside world shines through Carla's words that was barely appreciable during therapy. This curiosity confirms her recovery of a more appropriate developmental space which is less invaded by family burdens and conflicts. Her curiosity also indirectly reflects changes in the relationships that have occurred between the other family members, who have "permitted" Carla to return to her adolescent dilemmas.

Carla can now look at the vicissitudes of her anorectic illness with more detachment, asking herself questions about the past with greater objectivity and facing a future about which she is more uncertain, but also more hopeful of being able "to come back to life." Carla can now look forward and the future appears to be less confused with the present.

We should feel satisfied if the image of Don Quixote, suggested by the therapist in the most critical moments of therapy, continues to puzzle her after a few years. This is a vital image, still laden with meanings and questions to which Carla can provide her own answers. She will have different answers at different times, as her needs and her awareness of herself and of others change.

From the experience of one family's therapy which was long-lasting and deeply felt by all, Carla emerges with a *me* ("thanks for not forgetting about me") that is strong and distinct, confirming that the best outcome of therapy is to restore to each person a clearer sense of his or her own identity.

THE EVOLUTION TOWARD
OTHER FORMS OF THERAPY

The awareness that successful family therapy can produce a rupture in the schemata of repetitive and unchanging relationships and foster a process of greater individuation in each of its members leads us to consider the evolution toward other forms of therapy as a positive result (Andolfi & Angelo, 1985b).

In our clinical practice, for example, we quite frequently get requests for individual therapy from the identified patient or one of the family members. In the latter case, it is usually the person who was most insistent to begin family therapy. The request sometimes comes soon after the termination of family therapy and sometimes years later. It is understandable enough that the identified patient, once freed from his function as a pillar of the interpersonal tensions and conflicts of his family, can regain the capacity to make autonomous choices and therefore to ask for individual therapy. Especially if we are dealing with an adolescent or a young adult, a request for individual therapy can correspond to his emotional disengagement from the family. The family implicitly confirms his need to acquire his own personal space by "permitting" him to ask for something for himself. The opposite route of family therapy resulting from "successful" individual treatment appears to be much more difficult.

Some authors have observed (Boszormenyi-Nagy, 1987; Piperno, 1979) and described with different images, such as "undifferentiated family ego mass" (Bowen, 1966; see Simon, Stierlin, & Wynne, 1985; pp. 366–367) or "enmeshment" (Minuchin, 1974; see Simon, Stierlin, & Wynne, 1985, pp. 108–110), a sort of family sediment or lava. In such families, it is improbable that a patient who has serious symptoms can separate his own behavior and emotions from the confused network of family relationships and bonds that envelop him. Therefore, an individual intervention in this phase of collective fusion would be easily reabsorbed by a rigid family system, incapable of tolerating situations of approach (intimacy) and withdrawal (separation). A confirmation of this is the fact that many families with an adolescent or young adult identified patient arrive with a previous history of individual treatments that were unproductive and prematurely interrupted.[4]

Another very common outcome is that family therapy leads to couple therapy. This is frequent when the identified patient is a young child. The child's symptoms then represent the easiest opportunity to request outside help. At times the child's problems are so magnified or are presented with such alarm by the parents, as to really act as a safety valve to control explosive tensions that surely do not originate with the

---

[4]In some cases family therapy is requested by individual psychotherapists as "support" for their individual work, a situation that, with Selvini Palazzoli and Prata (1982), we consider to be a "snare" to a workable start of family therapy. The coexistence of different types of psychotherapy is a delicate and complex issue, a discussion of which would require much more space and goes beyond the scope of this chapter.

child. It is possible that by the parents being used as the main therapeutic resource in taking care of the child, they are reassured about their capacities to resolve their own relationship problems together, without a third party who acts as a "ground."

At the end of the family treatment, especially after having understood the relational meaning of the child's illness, it is possible that the spouses will present a more specific request, which now concerns their relationship as a couple explicitly. This outcome might be very different if the therapist, acting as the advocate for helpless children, sought to shift the problem from the child to the couple prematurely, instead of using the child's symptom to let the parents regain confidence in themselves and in their resources.

Simplifying the discussion, we can describe a progression from a maximal relational confusion to a maximal individual awareness. Family treatment, centered on the problems of the child or an adolescent, precedes an intervention in which the unit of observation is the couple, while the choice of going into therapy *alone* expresses a more mature capacity to search for answers to personal needs.

The sequence that follows and concludes this chapter exemplifies what we have said about the evolution from family treatment to individual therapy for the identified patient. The dialogue is taken from a follow-up session, held three years after the conclusion of family therapy. Participating in the session besides Lella's family are the family therapist, Dr. Andolfi (indicated as "Therapist"), and the individual therapist, Dr. Gemma Trepanese (indicated as "Individual Therapist"), who followed the girl in weekly sessions for two years.

Lella presents as a lovely 18-year-old adolescent, physically well groomed and with graceful gestures. She is in her first year of studies at ISEF (Higher Institute of Physical Education). To see her today, it would be difficult to believe that she has a history of serious childhood depression, accompanied by symptoms of anorexia nervosa starting at puberty and lasting several years. Her two younger sisters, Laura and Giorgia, are equally gracious, and her parents seem decidedly more lively. In particular, the father appears ten years younger and dresses in a sporty fashion. In the course of the family sessions he had been continually teased by his wife and three daughters for his gloomy tone which made him sound older.

The wife arrives with a kitten in her arms (the latest member of the family), calm and full of kindness and understanding. She seems to have given up the part of the "silly goose" which she frequently personified in the course of therapy, as if to balance the husband's part as an annoyed and "moldy" old man.

We are now towards the end of the meeting:

Therapist: Lella, what help do you think you received when you were having more problems and you used to come to Rome with your family? And what help do you feel you received later, continuing in therapy alone in Naples?

Lella: Maybe the work in Rome served as a passkey for the later work . . .

Mother (energetically) In Rome she got "unblocked"!

Father: Lella, did you ask yourself why you got unblocked in Rome?

Lella: Why? I don't know . . .

Therapist: Lella, would you have been able to go into therapy with Dr. Trepanese right away, before coming to Rome?

Mother: (doubtful) Alone? Then?

Lella: No, I really don't think so.

Therapist: Why not?

Lella: I could only manage to talk with a lot of effort, then . . . I really don't think so . . .

Therapist: What do you say, Signora, would she have been able to, right away?

Mother: She wouldn't have come at all. We were all so entangled and Lella was at the center of the tangle.

Father: First of all, we should say that she had started individual psychotherapy with Professor Bianchi, a psychiatrist in Naples . . . but it just didn't work.

Mother: In fact, he insisted that she stop therapy with him, because we had begun our family meetings in Rome.

Therapist: If you had to give advice to a family that finds itself in a situation similar to yours five years ago, what would you advise them?

Mother: I recommended family therapy to several of our friends with similar problems, and I would always recommend family therapy!!

Father: Family therapy. I'm judging by the results. Lella got unblocked really by coming to Rome and we have understood so many of our mistakes . . . so many of our fears. I came here today reluctantly, I would have preferred to cancel, but these meetings meant so much to Lella, so . . .

Therapist: Well, I remember that our sessions were very hard for everybody . . . so much suffering . . . all locked up in Lella's stomach . . . enough to make you burst . . .

Mother: I understood what happened here in Rome, but I don't know how to put it into words. . . . There was an initial unblocking for Lella, for all of us. . . . Do you remember the session about the corks? I've often thought about all the corks that I put on my fears . . . it was a little like a plough that keeps going over hard ground and turning up the earth. Certainly, individual therapy has been very important for Lella, it's been her own space . . . that was necessary at that point, because before that she was almost dead spiritually . . .

Lella: (without conviction) Yeah, well, just like now, more or less . . . confused . . .

Individual Therapist: Now you have problems as a confused adolescent; before, as an anorectic patient, you were spiritually dead. . . . Now I feel there is a new possibility for Lella to *get closer* to Father, Mother, Laura, Giorgia, while

after the meetings in Rome, maybe your biggest temptation was to run far away.

Father: See how strange life is? . . . Now we've "run away" to
Modena (*the father was transferred a few years ago to Modena
by his bank in Naples*) and Lella has taken our place in
Naples.

Therapist: So the adults have finally grown up and left home,
leaving room for the adolescents to grow up!

Individual Therapist: And yet, in spite of the physical distance,
now I feel that Lella has found the courage to get close
to her parents, to make demands on them. (*facing the father*) When you were speaking a minute ago, you were
watching Lella and I noticed a different look, a new
curiosity . . .

Lella: (*a little embarrassed*) Papa, don't look at me like that
now. . . . You're turning red all over (*the father cries, cov-
ering his eyes*) . . . I've never seen him cry.

Therapist: There's always a time to see your father crying . . .

Lella: I'm happy because usually you feel embarrassed when
you see a man crying.

Father: Female weakness, eh?

Lella: When I cry, I feel weak too . . . but seeing Papa crying
now is different . . .

Therapist: You mean that this is also a form of intimacy . . .
I'm also pleased to see him crying, he's more alive . . .
now the moldy old trunk from the attic has been dusted
off. The trip to Modena has really been useful.

Father: To make me cry, eh?

Therapist: See how funny we are in this world!

Father: (*amused*) Yes, really! Such clowns . . . !

Therapist: Fine. Well, good luck!

CHAPTER 8

The Myth of Atlas:
A Therapeutic Story
in Progress

A CASE STUDY BY
DR. MARCELLA DE NICHILO[1]

In the first chapter we were introduced to the Penna family who were brought to therapy by Lucio, the family organizer. They are a family consisting of a widowed mother and her eight children who present themselves as tight as a football huddle.

Our clinic records show that a year before, the mother had contacted the Institute of Family Therapy in Rome by telephone to schedule a family session, but that subsequently the appointment was cancelled because the family was unable to convince Dino, the identified patient, to attend the session. A year later it is his brother Lucio who calls the therapist to make a new appointment. That is how we come to know that Dino, who had already presented a major crisis the previous year, "was admitted to a psychiatric hospital for a confusional state." Among other irrational behaviors, "he burned his

---

[1]This chapter is a clinical elaboration of some theoretical ideas on the evolution of myths in family therapy developed in a paper by Dr. Marcella de Nichilo (de Nichilo, 1986)

mother's mattress" and seems also to have had problems with drugs and ill-defined "mental lapses." The mother, Lucia, a vigorous woman of 59, who works in a municipal office in Palermo, Sicily, has eight children. Gino, who is 35 and married with three children, has moved out. Elena, 33, is married, lives with her husband and six-year-old son, is a college graduate, and works as a teacher. Mario, 32, who works as a technician, is married, and has a child of two and lives with his own family. Lucio, 28, unemployed, gave up his studies in economics and business three years ago to live at home. Caterina, 25, has a degree and is about to marry but still lives with the family. Dino, the identified patient, is 22 and has interrupted his college studies. Livio, 19, and Andrea, 17, are in school but are having academic problems. The last two children live at home with Dino, Caterina and Lucio, and are all supported by the mother.[2] (See Figure 8.1 for a genogram of the Penna family.)

A FATHER BY CALLING

In the first session, the therapist, remembering his telephone conversation with Lucio who initiated therapy, begins by gathering information, for the most part without antagonizing the family's self-image or their myth of harmony and union. The therapist looks into the relevance or the function of Lucio's role as acting father, examining what supports it, what opposes it, and how.

Lucio: (declaring his concern for everybody) Business . . . office things, Dino, and the problems of the little kids.

---

[2]The therapy was conducted by Dr. Maurizio Andolfi for 13 sessions in the course of a clinical seminar, with a group of observers behind the mirror. The sessions were held monthly from the first to the ninth session. Subsequently, there were longer intervals: three months between the ninth and tenth sessions; four months between the eleventh (which included a special consultation by Dr. Carl Whitaker) and twelfth sessions; and an interval of two months between the twelfth and thirteenth session. After about a year there was a telephone follow-up by Dr. Andolfi with the family in Palermo, and further follow-up conversations in succeeding years.

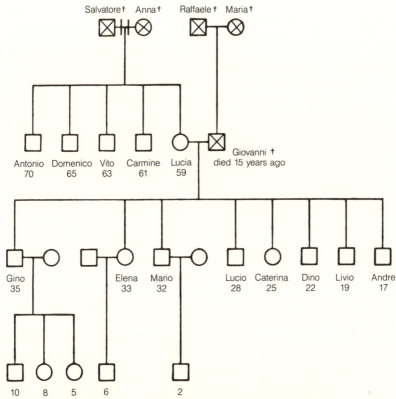

Figure 8.1. Genogram of the Penna family.

Therapist: And who are the little kids? (*Livio and Andrea stand up. They are 5'7" and 5'11" tall, respectively. Roaring laughter all around. Therapist laughs along with them.*) I understand. Well, I won't make all of you stand up. I just wanted to see. (*turning to Lucio*) But do you get a salary for all this?

Lucio: No, not really.

Therapist: It's voluntary, then. (*turning then to the three older children, he takes some history to gather new information about the family roles and functions*) Before getting married, did any of you act as father in his place?

Mother: No.

Mario: No, I've been married three years.

Therapist: So, before Lucio you acted as father . . .

Mother: (quickly) No, no, he wasn't up to it.

Therapist: He didn't pay his dues to the family?

Mother: He wasn't interested, he studied, went out with his friends. He just wasn't interested in the little kids. Lucio, on the other hand, involved himself with his brothers and sisters.

Therapist: Wait a minute, wasn't "father" interested in everybody, not just the little kids. Actually, how many are living at home?

The therapist now begins to establish differences between the biological father (father to all) and the pseudo-father who wants to be father only to the so-called "little kids." This allows Mario to act from the beginning as co-therapist, openly questioning the apparent authority of mother and Lucio, who stumble along in daily life.

Mario: Every day we hear complaints, especially from this fellow here, my brother (*indicating Lucio*).

Therapist: About what?

Mario: About food; always complaining. "The meat is burnt," "the pasta is cold," and the others follow him, always complaining. And my mother, to keep the peace, gets up and cooks him an omelette or cutlet, anything to please him.

Lucio, who at the outset presented himself as a "father by calling," is beginning to be devalued by Mario's words. Mario's description of the confusion that regularly occurs at mealtimes at home reveals Lucio's incompetence as the family head and sheds light on the inconsistency of his authority when acting as father. This information, revealed through a series of questions by the therapist, makes explicit from the first session the internal mutiny against Lucio's authority, forcing him to explode and to declare his defeat.

Lucio: I wasn't elected. I took over and that's it. Andrea, Livio, and Caterina don't interfere. Dino leaves me alone . . . my mother does what I say, so I'm in charge!

Lucio's declaration of impotence about any real power in the family will also permit the mother to show her own weariness over having tried to be both mother and father after the death of her husband, without receiving any recognition from her children. For years mother had expected solidarity and support, especially from her oldest daughter, Elena. However, after the death of her father, Elena challenges her mother's role as a "total parent" in the father's mold.

Elena: Mama has an independent personality, she's authoritarian. What she has in mind must be done. Maybe we're both authoritarian, but I'm on very good terms with my brothers. She's nervous and demanding above all; she makes scenes when the bills arrive . . . even when Papa was alive. (*turning to mother*) I wanted you to be much closer to all of us, for understanding, for affection. Instead you always have to do it your way. This is what got you into trouble with all of us.

Mother: And I have to pay. I raised them all by myself.

Therapist: For how many years?

Mother: For 15 years, since my husband died.

Therapist: And when did Lucio enter as the new father?

Mother: In the last few months.

Elena: Mother said for a few months. That's not true. It's at least two years.

Lucio: For two years I've been doing everything. Anyway, for a year now, things have gotten a little more complicated.

Lucio's resentment mirrors mother's resentment in not feeling supported or appreciated for his hard work. Lucio has failed, succeeding neither inside nor outside the family. In fact he not only abandoned university to assist his siblings and his family, but also, due to Dino's problems, lost an office job he had worked hard to earn. Electing himself to act as father, he attempted an impossible task: to fill the large void left by his father, who was not only loved in life, but idealized after his premature death. The mother also failed in her attempt to play the role of a supercompetent total parent and only ended up being incapable of reaching her children. The result of all this is a ritual wherein the more she acts like the family pillar, the more her children see her as an aloof, distant woman who does not seem to need them.

Elena: Papa was a pillar, because first of all he was a man who knew how to understand children.

Lucio also appears to be a failure compared to the exalted image of the father. He not only fails to resemble his father but ends up making father appear to have been a tyrant. In this way, one of the family's salient characteristics emerges: their unclear perception of the hierarchy of values for which the father, Giovanni, acted as a pillar, while in the current situation, there is only a void in his place. (In the third session, Dino will say, "This pillar is a plain . . . a plain divided into so many parts.") The children who are now considered the "big kids" were adolescents 15 years ago and at a flexible stage of development when they lost their father ("In only two months he was gone!"), struck by stomach cancer. The "little kids," on the other hand, only knew him as infants, or at a more emotionally dependent stage when they had not yet developed a critical sense. It is not accidental then that Dino, who constitutes the generational breakwater between the older siblings and the younger ones, carries the symptom.

The more the family myth of the father is magnified and embellished in memory as the one who knows (*Therapist:* "Who was Papa?" *Everybody:* "Papa knew"), the more Dino assumes the role of "the one who does not know," perpetuating his memory with the opposite image.

Therapist: I understand, so you're the one in the family who belongs and doesn't belong.

Dino: Well, yes.

Therapist: So your family came here for you?

Dino: Um, I don't know.

Therapist: If you don't know . . .

Dino: I found myself here unexpectedly.

Therapist: Unexpectedly? How did they tell you?

Dino: That we had to go for a visit to see someone.

Therapist: To go for a visit, like this, like going for coffee?

Dino: No, to talk a bit about the family.

Therapist: And who told you?

Dino: Everybody told me a bit.

Therapist: In such an ambiguous way?

Dino: Uh-hah.

Therapist: Why do they have to tell you things in such an ambiguous way?

Dino: Um, I don't know.

Therapist: Then you are the smallest of the little kids?

Dino: Could be.

With his confused attitude, Dino is trying to keep the group together, playing the part of an irresponsible person and blocking his own growth and everyone else's by freezing time, which seems to have stopped for everybody in the legendary time when the father was alive. Moreover, by avoiding a direct and painful confrontation with his own failures, Dino avoids taking charge of his own life in the here and now.

THE FAMILY IS "TOO NARROW"

The therapist gets the message of incompetence and extreme disorganization sent out by the family and begins to look for a preliminary plausible hypothesis (Ugazio, 1984). He shifts his inquiry onto a trigenerational plane.

Therapist: So not only your husband died, but your family of origin died too.

Mother: Exactly, yes.

Therapist: How did all these people die?

Mother: My husband was an only child. His father, Raffaele, wanted many children. In fact, after 15 years of marriage when no one expected it anymore, he was born. And his mother, Maria, what she suffered! Those days in Sicily, if a woman didn't have children it's as if she were good for nothing . . . better not to have been born!

Therapist: Well, then, he didn't like being an only child.

Mother: He used to say, I don't want to have an only child.

Therapist: So now you have a family of your own . . . and when Giovanni died, he left you this heritage! They are all children of your husband?

Mother: (*emphatically*) All children of the same father. As a matter of fact . . . (*with sadness*) eight kids and six miscarriages . . .

Therapist: You weren't prepared for this "team" of children!

Mother: No, he wanted the children because he was an only child. He wanted them to have brothers and sisters so they wouldn't be alone in the world like he was. Me instead, coming from a large family I didn't want so many of them . . . if I hadn't had those miscarriages now there would be 14!

Therapist: (*to Lucio*) You didn't tell me anything about your mother's history. (*to the mother*) You know, I am amazed that it wasn't you who called me on the telephone, Signora Penna. After five minutes I finally understood that Lucio wasn't your husband and then I felt confused.

By making Lucio's bogus function as father more clear, the therapist can allow the mother's loneliness, which had been hidden behind her worries about Dino, to emerge.

Mother: The fact is that I feel too exhausted in this situation. Dino goes out and doesn't come back, sometimes for days . . . At night I can't get to sleep, I have palpitations of my heart. I don't know what to do about things like . . . drugs.

This change of context permits the mother to show her suffering—"I'm not a rock, I'm a woman, exhausted and alone." Now the therapist may challenge the rigidity of the system more openly, contrasting the mythical time experienced by the family with the meaningfulness of therapeutic time, directing questions at the here and now.

Therapist: Signora, do you want to help me?

Mother: Certainly, that's what I'm here for, to find a way out of this situation with my son.

Therapist: I feel that this family is too "narrow" . . . for me, there are too few people . . . or there are too many of the same type. If you want to help me, you must bring here, besides your children, some of your siblings.

Mother: I don't know, I can't say, since I don't see them.

Therapist: How many years did you live in Palermo with your siblings?

Mother: Twenty years, until I got married.

Therapist: Signora, if you want to help me, you'll have to bring at least one of your siblings, to let me understand how things were going before Papa's death. How many siblings do you have?

Mother: Four. I'm the only daughter.

Therapist: What are your brothers' names? Where do they live?

Mother: Antonio lives in Sicily, but he's paralyzed. Domenico also has a large family. Vito lives in Milan. Carmine works in Venezuela. I can't bother them.

Therapist: And nobody helped you when Dino was ill?

Mother: Vito's daughter kept him at her house in the North for some months, but then, just when he got sick again

(*he had returned home*), she got married. I didn't go to the
wedding. How could I go to her wedding when my son
was so sick? And she was offended . . .

Therapist: I can't believe that none of your four brothers is pre-
pared to help you. You should say to them: "I went to a
doctor in Rome. I want help with Dino's problem who
acts crazy. I need your help."

Mother: If they don't come, I can't make them . . .

Therapist: If you don't help me, I can't go on. *Don't let any
of your children help you,* this is something between you
and me.

The aim of the therapist is to help each member of the family regain more appropriate generational positions, therefore
pushing Dino, who poses as the one who has been displaced
in the family's mythical time, to regain his own space in his
own time. Such an operation is possible if the therapist has
successfully established a collaborative relationship with the
mother on two levels at the same time, treating the mother as
a responsible adult and seeing her in the context of her family
story.

In the subsequent sessions, the presence first of Domenico
("He's not the most important, but the easiest one to bring
along"), whom the therapist seats beside the mother in Lucio's place, and then of Vito, who came just at the right moment from Milan ("The brother who is most dear to me"),
allows an exploration of mother's relationship with her family
of origin. Such presences will bring about modifications of
rigid and preconceived functions, constructing a new history
in the context of therapy.

In this way, we will discover that the mother's current behavior "preserves" her heritage. Her grudge against men
comes from her family of origin. Her father, Salvatore, "used
to hit his wife" because she complained that he was a wom-
anizer and absent, neglecting his children and making everyone feel ashamed and hopeless.

Domenico: My father never separated from my mother . . .
only when he found a new lock on the door of the house
that my brother Carmine had installed did he understand that we were throwing him out. He knocked at another door and went to live with a cheap woman. But my
mother was a decent person!

Gino: (interjecting and looking at Mrs. Penna) My mother has
suffered a lot. She never forgot the wrong that was done
to her, even when she was left a widow. She rolled up
her sleeves and slaved night and day. Mama was the one
who even helped me find work. And I won't forget it.
But I still feel she was hard on Papa.

The pain and the humiliation of their father's irresponsible
behavior was so great that Lucia, Dino's mother, was not
present at his funeral, as a sign of her unending grudge
against him, reflecting a rigid Sicilian moral code. Moreover,
since Dino was sick, she no longer attended weddings and
festive occasions of friends and relatives, to the point of not
being involved even in the approaching wedding of her own
daughter, Caterina, as if getting married was a calamity. The
information about the family history given by her brothers allows us to enter Lucia's emotional world. Her sense of being
an orphan, her distrust of relationships with men, and the
solidarity of her relationship with her mother, who felt deeply
betrayed, had prevented Lucia from asking help from her
brothers, even at the most critical moments. She feared that
even they, like her father, would confuse authority with violence and would beat the nephews and nieces if they made
mistakes, abusing their authority. The testimony of the uncles
not only allows Lucia to appear as a *mother hen rather than a
rock*, but also starts to depict Giovanni, the dead father, as less
charismatic and more human, first through the words of Domenico and then those of mother herself.

Domenico: My nephews and nieces had too much freedom for
my taste. It was mostly my brother-in-law who gave

them freedom. And then my sister followed in her husband's wake. I would have done it my way . . .

Therapist: And what would your way have been?

Domenico: Putting a brake on all this freedom even by force.
My sister is right when she says that I'm a bit of a
tyrant . . . when she was alone at home I had her in my
control. But my nephew Gino is wrong when he says
that his mother is tough. Because my sister has a soft
spot for children that's excessive, as she had maybe even
for her husband. Maybe she loved him more than she
says. The fact is that when a person is reserved, if she is
hurt, she starts to be bossy . . . as a cover-up.

Vito: My sister is tired, I've never seen her as tired as she is
now. She can't take it anymore.

As the mother gets more support, her depression becomes
more evident.

Mother: When I got married I was 20 years old. After two
months our marriage was already a failure. The gossip
came after. I got to know Giovanni when he was in the
army. [Military service is compulsory for all Italian
men—Trans.] He was very attached to his mother,
Maria. He wanted to give her lots of grandchildren before she died. I had left him because of a lie. Then a
neighbor intruded and my mother made things worse:
"He's a good boy!" In short, after three months we were
married. It was fate.

Therapist: And the gossip?

Mother: He knew how to talk, he was a perfect talker. But he
told lies. I like the truth, I'm frank.

Therapist: In what sense did you find him false?

Mother: He would buy, let's say, something for a hundred
thousand lire [about $100—Trans.]. He would tell me it
cost fifty thousand lire [about $50—Trans.]. How would I

find out? He would sign and later the bills would arrive. The police would come to seize our furniture. It isn't a nice thing, you know. But he brought home gifts for the children!

IMAGINARY ILLNESSES AND REAL VOIDS

This exploration through time of a physical and moral death arising in each generation in the form of fate induces a growing distress in Dino, who for the first time can talk about his own illness more explicitly, although still enigmatically.

Dino: My problem is this: I've got humanitarian problems. Therefore, I lack organs . . . physical ones.

Therapist: Excuse me, what do you mean by "physical organs"?

Dino: I talked about it to my family.

Therapist: Is this absence hard on you? On you or on someone else in the family?

Dino: No, it's not hard, but I have to find the words.

Therapist: Is there someone in the family who can help you? Today your uncle helped your mother . . . (*turning to Mario*) Can you help your brother?

Mario: I can try. (*turning to Dino*) Physical organs are arms, legs, ears, your nose. Are they missing?

Dino: No, wait. I'm referring more than anything to abstract organs.

Mario: You mean, the soul, thought . . . ?

Elena: Conscience?

Therapist: Are you worried that you are missing some physical organ?

Dino: Yes, but not on the material level, on a more abstract plane.

Therapist: Are any of you worried that you are missing anything physical?

Mario: It's not a question of missing something. I think that
    he's had kidney trouble since he was little.

In this way, a long story unfolded about illnesses: first Dino's glomerulonephritis (a kidney infection) at age six; then
Lucio, who had a kidney and his spleen removed after a car
accident, and Gino, who was born with a heart murmur; and,
finally, the father's fatal cancer. The family is inclined to exor-
cise their fear of death, speaking of illnesses superficially, like
things of little consequence, denying their seriousness.

Therapist: (to the mother) But does Dino know these things?
Mother: No.
Therapist: (to Dino) Didn't they ever tell you these things?
Dino: No, but I heard rumors.
Therapist: Talking very seriously or like talking about the flu?
Dino: Like this, the way we tell stories in the family, like
    a pastime.

The symbolic implications of Dino's nonverbal language
now become more decipherable as his symbiotic relationship
with his family becomes explicit. His distress becomes the
whole family's distress. Only by throwing light on who the
father really was, through the mother's testimony, is it possible for the therapist to give substance to the void that Dino,
with his strange behavior, and Lucio, with his pretense of being father, are vainly trying to fill up. The family's conspiracy
of silence concerning the taboo about death not only hinders
an exchange of mutual help, but also reinforces the stereotype
of "weak" men as physical and social failures compared to
"strong" women who, in spite of endless obstacles, following
the example of the women of previous generations, succeed
through willpower to keep themselves whole and face their
difficulties.

It seems that the script of the family myth assigns to the
males the paradoxical task of asserting their own existence

only as symbols and not as real persons. That is how it was for the father—alive, he was a failure; in death, he acquired greatness and respect. The same happened to Lucio who follows in his father's footsteps, and to the other men in the family who have had serious difficulties both at home and beyond. Dino expresses his distress with his perpetual oscillations between the real and the imaginary, with uncertain assertions about his own illnesses, precariously balanced between the physical and the abstract. Only with the concrete presence of someone who acts as an intermediary between the real and the imaginary, helping him to reconstruct the missing script as well as everybody's boundaries, will he be able to interrupt this game of mirrors in which one can recognize one's own image only through that of a nonexistent other.

Therapist: What would have happened if Papa was alive?
Dino: I don't know, I think it would have been different.
Therapist: How?
Mario: Better or worse?
Dino: I think I would have stayed in school.

To permit Dino to free himself from his role as a "hinge" in the family and to be what he is—a young man with typical problems for his age—the therapist must use himself as a model of flexibility, entering and leaving the therapy room, now to join the family, now to meet with the observers behind the mirror. His play of entering and leaving symbolically represents "presence" within "nonpresence," which until now has allowed the myth to be perpetuated. Now a new way is proposed to the rigid organization of the family: *family members are to negotiate how to help each other.* If Dino recognizes the hurt that his silence causes him, he will be ready to "come out into the open," instead of paralyzing the family with his dilemma of what is true and what is not (for example, his use of drugs). The more Dino refuses to clarify his symptoms, the more the therapist makes concrete requests, assigning structural tasks that tend to redefine the generational boundaries.

These redefinitions are made possible by the presence of the uncles as *consultants*. Their presence permits a redrawing of more adequate lines of authority and at the same time implies a concrete undertaking that stresses a newly found unity within the extended family. In this way the mother's responsibility becomes progressively deemphasized and she is sent away on vacation for three weeks, to relax with her brother Domenico, while Elena and Lucio will act as parents, even managing the family's finances, under the supervision of the uncles who are now seen as reliable.

While the mother is away, each of her children must plan some project together with his or her younger sibling, doing some practical jobs for which they are responsible (cleaning the walls of the house, for example), using the simple and direct language of Mario, who for several sessions has acted as co-therapist. The mother must thus give up her control of the money to the acting parents and take care of herself. Dino will not be allowed to get lost in his philosophical meanderings and must use his knowledge of street life to guide his unemployed younger brother, Andrea, to find work, replacing their old game based on rigid roles with a new experience of competence. The therapist's interventions are aimed at an emotional reorganization of the family based on a trigenerational model. He introduces the image of a soccer team in crisis.

Therapist: I feel unable to help you, if this means hunting for your mother's real or imagined faults. I can't step into Giovanni's shoes either, which I couldn't fill anyway. I believe I can help you to see and to become aware of the "bad plays" in this family. It's like a soccer team that loses even if it's united. It loses not because the players aren't good, but because their plays are wrong, or because their positions on the field are wrong.

With the metaphor of a scoreless game, the therapist does not accept failure as the family's "fate." Offering himself as a coach, he challenges the family to learn a more productive team game, provided that each person observes the rules of the new game that will be played in each session. The fifth session closes with the promise to bring to the next session family pictures in which the father is present, in order to help the therapist to know what Giovanni looked like.

DINO'S ABSENCE AND
THE THERAPIST'S LETTER

At the sixth session Dino is absent. His physical absence parallels his father's absence from the photo album. This is mirrored by the mother's confusing Dino with her late husband.

Therapist: (referring to Giovanni's photos) This man, the one in your hand, does he haunt you?
Mother: Who, Dino?
Therapist: The man who's in the picture in your hand.
Mother: I don't understand. He locks himself up in his room, he might come to the table, sit down, eat, and run away. Or he'll ask for money, for a sweater, for cigarettes . . . and squander it.

The therapist blocks the usual rigmarole over the strange ways of Dino who is not present, trying to shed light on the father's presence in the family through the testimony of the photographs. This interaction confirms the image of the father as a ghost in a fantasy relationship with the mother. Dino's absence when they talk about the death of the father now becomes clear as a camouflage maneuver.

Therapist: But who's the key person in these pictures?
Mother: (acting confused) The key person here? Well, there's my husband, in another sense there's me, but for the time

being the key person is Dino. We feel sorry and we're
sacrificing for this boy.

Therapist: My dear lady, maybe I'm suffering from amnesia
too . . . who were these pictures supposed to let us see?

Mother: I don't know . . . you said to bring in pictures of *before*
and *after* my husband's death . . . those that we managed to find.

Therapist: Who is the key person in the picture?

Mother: Nobody, because it's the group (*this confirms the symbiotic structure of the family*).

Therapist: But, are you sure he's dead?

Mother: Who, Dino?

Therapist: Dino is alive, if he didn't die last night.

Mother: Died . . . who? The person missing from my house
is . . . my father-in-law, wait—no, no, the one who's
missing is my husband.

Therapist: Will you show me a picture of your husband?

Mother: (*flipping through the album*) Here's the whole family,
but it's a bad shot. Here's Andrea. Here's my father.
Here's Livio. . . . (*with a sad and slightly frustrated look*)
There aren't any pictures of my husband alone.

Therapist: Giovanni seems to me more of a ghost than a dead
husband who's resting in peace . . . I'm very confused,
because this session was all centered on Papa and it
seems that nobody can show me what he looked like.
Let's talk about it.

Lucio: Well, it's very hard to talk about it.

Therapist: Maybe the first failure in the family was him?

Mother: A failed man?

Lucio: Maybe so, because he certainly didn't like the work he
did . . . actually, it's true that he left it and started a new
career, as a salesman for a drug company. Then he used
to say, "If I hadn't made so many mistakes! To start with,
I wouldn't have married and I would have studied." He
was always telling us, "Study and you'll be better off
in life."

Therapist: But in fact he wasn't able to study himself . . .

Lucio: No.

Therapist: He failed.

Lucio: He failed because his father had died and left him alone with his widowed mother, an only child. And then with the war, they had lost everything.

Therapist: I'm asking myself if this man is still a ghost, because in flesh and blood he was a failure.

Lucio: This is how you tell men apart in Sicily: man, half-man, and *quaquaracquà.*[3] Who knows if Papa was a man or half a man? . . .

Mother: Yes, he had an "easy hand," passing out bad checks.

Livio: But it was him who bought the country house . . . for us, with his savings.

Therapist: What house?

Livio: A little place beside the sea. The house in Palermo instead was . . . a tomb.

Andrea: A nice house. In the country. And the trees, so many trees, one by one Papa planted them before he died.

Mother: He bought it, because I like the ocean so much. In '67 we signed the contract, in '69 we started building.

Lucio: And we completed it, putting in all the finishing touches.

Elena and Caterina: With joy.

Therapist: Well done!

The half-hidden face of the father in the family pictures allows us to dig beyond myth into historical reality. This uncovers a real man with good and bad parts. The photographs act as a transitional object. The family can now face its contradictory reality with less certainty, but also avoid idealization as well as devaluation, as used to be the case.

Dino is absent again in the following session.

---

[3] An expression in Sicilian slang meaning "braggart" or "boaster."

Lucio: Dino is at the station.

Therapist: At the station?

Mother: He came as far as Rome and then stayed back at the station.

Therapist: So he wanted you to come here?

The therapist gives positive meaning and value to his absence: if until this point Dino was used as a cover for family conflicts, his absence can help to uncover the embarrassment that each person feels now that it's clear who and what Papa really was.

Lucio: (tensely) I am calm.

Therapist: There are people who are sick and don't make a fuss, there are people like Dino who are sick and make a fuss, and there are people who are sick and can't admit it. And I'm not talking about only men or women . . . both sexes.

Mother: I am very sick.

Livio: It's difficult to be a man if your father is half a man. . . . You can lose some battles, but it's important to win the war. . . . Lately I've been thinking a lot about everything and it bothers me.

Therapist: If you didn't have Dino, where would you put all these problems and emotions?

Lucio: I feel I'm Lucio. I feel like a man . . . and sometimes I feel at peace, peaceful but hopeless.

Therapist: (leaves the therapy room and returns after a while with a letter which he hands to Livio) This is a letter which you will give to Dino. You've been a big help to me today, thank you.

Livio has helped the therapist to reshape the image of the phantom father into a living human being, using the metaphor of the father as "half a man." The therapist provides an image mirroring Livio's wordplay, handing him a cryptic letter for Dino. This introduces a new code to decipher.

This letter is read by Dino in person in the eighth session. At first Dino reads absentmindedly, like someone who does not understand and falters (there is a meaningful slip where he mispronounces *morti* which means "dead" as *molti* meaning "many"). Then he reads it correctly. This reading is an important marker of Dino's change from the identified patient to being a responsible person, reflecting the new developmental stage achieved by the whole family.

DR. ANDOLFI'S LETTER

Dear Dino:

Thank you for your help from a distance, helping me understand that in your family it is hard not to fail if Papa is half a man and the women are never self-critical about who they are. However, I am not at all sure that just because you are not here the others can say something about themselves—their fears and hopelessness—instead of thinking that your recovery will magically resolve everything. For the next session I would like the whole family to be here. Today Livio helped me understand that one can die peacefully or die upset or just die, just because one doesn't have the courage to live.

THE MEALTIME RITUAL AND
THE GAME OF THREE CARDS

Dino's presence in the eighth session confirms to the therapist his availability to act as a regulator of the therapeutic process. After eight months of therapy Dino appears not only to be able to tolerate the void he had been left with when father died, but no longer to have a need to defend his father in front of everybody, complaining as he did in the fifth session of "being the little one" (*Dino laughs at this*). He now knows, as the others do, what the game is about. Turning to Dino as the medium for the whole therapeutic system, the therapist asks the family to enact their mealtime ritual in the session. It is already known that at mealtimes big arguments break out between Lucio and his siblings and between mother and Dino. What is not known yet is *where* all these arguments break out. What becomes clear is that in the dining room where the arguments occur is where Papa lay ill in the last months of his life. The room, then, has a sacred function as the father's sanctuary. Now that he is dead, Dino plays the role of "guardian of this tomb," lying on the same sofa where Papa used to lay and preventing everybody from having their meals in peace. They are unable to change their associations with this room from the functions of illness and death to those of nutrition and life.

Therapist: (to Dino) Will you show me, using this room, how you eat together in Palermo?

Dino: What do you mean, "eat"?

Therapist: Can you show me what happens?

Gino: (referring to Dino) He's usually slouching on the couch . . .

Therapist: Oh! Here we need a mat . . . here we are (*he takes a rubber mat from a cupboard*). Now would you like to sit at the table like you do at home?

Mother (turning to Dino as she is sitting down at the table) He rejects me.

Therapist: I want to understand what happens in this family.

Mother: I must say I can't. It's too hard.

Therapist: Signora, you don't have to talk, just act. You others, all of you, can help to construct the scene. I need to understand if Dino is still a baby, sucking for milk, if he's lazy and doesn't want to do anything with himself, or if he's crazy. I still haven't figured out which of these hypotheses is the right one (*the therapist leaves*).

The three hypotheses about who Dino is, "baby, lazy, or crazy," re-echo the three possible interpretations about who Papa was: "man, half-man, or braggart." This verbal analogy is quickly caught by Dino. When his mother complains, "I tell him, 'I'll cook you a cutlet' and he pushes me away," Dino responds:

Dino: Mama, what the hell do you want? So what if I push you away? What, do we sleep together?

This statement explains how the tension of Dino's strange behavior, such as burning his mother's mattress, has an internal logic or rationale which is now more decipherable. This rationale will be exploded during the Andolfi-Whitaker consultation in the eleventh session.

Mother: Then why are you always lying around?
Dino: And what's it to you? What do you care if I lie in bed?
Mother: It's nothing to me, you just lie there thinking all the time. . . . (*a short silence*) What do you mean, "What's it to me?" I'm your mother.
Dino: What you have to do is to give me money and that's all! (*The therapist returns.*)
Therapist: Wait a minute, I want to get back to the meal. Show me all the little details. (*to Dino*) So you stay stretched out.
Livio: Here, Dino, come on, this is your bed.
Lucio: Dino, it's ready, come and eat! (I open the door, I tell him and then I go).
Mother: And how does he answer you?
Dino: I'm coming!
All: He says he's coming but he doesn't come.
Lucio: (*to mother*) Let's sit down! Dino told me he's coming. (*there's a bustle*)

Mother: (to Lucio) Where is he?

Lucio: On his bed, in the dark. Let's see if he comes. Get his plate ready!

Mother: His plate is ready.

Lucio: (to Andrea) Andrea, aren't you eating? There's your place.

Andrea: It's the same here.

Lucio: No, no, it's not the same thing. At home your place is there.

Dino: I'm eating. I'll put my glass here. Sometimes, however, I don't take a glass. Sometimes I eat my meal and sometimes I don't eat it.

Caterina: What do you say at times? "Make me an omelette!" They make it for you and you say, "I don't want it."

Lucio: When we're finished eating Dino gets up and goes back to bed.

Mother: He opens the windows and smokes.

Lucio: And starts to make an uproar.

Dino: (shouting) Give me money, Mama, don't bother me!

The scene now becomes hilarious. The tension dissolves with the outbreak of laughter by the family members, newly discovered actors who, more than just rehearsing their parts, enjoy playing their usual roles individually and together. They interpret their ambivalence about life and death, fiction and reality, with great skill. Through imitation and the "dramatis personae" (taking on roles played through masks) the context moves from tragedy to farce, thanks to the bisociative integration of the play.

The production of the usual ritual of the conflict that explodes and continues to explode at mealtime not only resounds in the arguments over money between mother and father, but also reevokes father's death without peace in the dining room. This induces Lucio to finally reveal *the deathbed secret* from Giovanni's mouth: *"If I survive, nobody will see me again; nobody will get help from me anymore, if I live."*

Elena: (shocked) What are you saying?

Lucio: I heard it myself. Look, maybe papa had had it with all of us, he was fed up with all of us . . .

Weariness and resentment are expressed in this way as circular problems that involved even the father before he died. Reediting the family drama introduces a new code for the testing and interpretation of what happened and continues to repeat itself in the light of recent events. This code is no longer cryptic as in the letter, but is now explicit. When Dino "sanely" recites his part as a "crazy," he allows himself and his family to reveal their usual interactions and to indicate more hidden truths, such as his ambivalent relationship with his mother.

It will be exactly through this nonverbal code that the family will show the level of learning it has achieved—that is, its capacity to project itself, through drama, into an alternative context to provide a creative reading of present and past facts with a freer, more critical, and more entertaining inventive language than the one that has now been made obsolete. An example of the family's assimilation of this new code is the highly original interpretation of the therapist's words in the following segment.

Therapist: (referring to Dino stretched out on the rubber mat) Now I understand, nobody knows anymore if this dead guy here is Dino or Papa . . . *(silent)*

Mother: He is called Dino-*Giovanni*. I understood that if Papa was "Giovanni Battista,"[4] Dino is "Giovanni Evangelista"[5] *(laughing)*.

The biblical reference is relevant to the extent that it indicates that mother can get rid of her armor and place herself in the perspective of an observer of herself and others instead of

---

[4] "John the Baptist."
[5] "John the Evangelist."

perpetuating her role of a priest who consecrates the ritual. If the function of father Giovanni was to gather disciples through his children, that of Dino-Giovanni is to instruct them to keep alive the *memento mori et resurrectionis*[6] with his symptom. This metaphorical figure, Dino-Giovanni, represents the point of intersection where multiple and even remote meanings flow into each other. This metaphor is the mother's chosen vehicle that allows the patient and the family to "leave home," that is, to leave their old roles in order to explore new ways of integrating the present into the future.

After eight months of therapy, the therapist's suggestion to play the game of "three cards" is made as a way of appraising how much has been achieved, especially the family's ability to face the complex problem of choice. In a changed context, where it seems that the old way of playing is no longer satisfying, a new, more entertaining game is proposed which contributes to modifying the overall meaning of Dino's behavior and the others' complementary behavior towards him.

This phase of metaphorical action, initiated with the humorous replay of the meal, continues in the next session when the patient and the family are invited by the therapist to play a card game. "Three cards" is a very popular game in Southern Italy, where the game is played with *imbroglio*[7] which makes it both entertaining and risky.

Everybody, including Dino, has to bet money each time on one of three cards. Written on each card is : Dino is a *baby*, Dino is *lazy*, or Dino is *crazy*. While the three players choose what to bet on, the three cards are skillfully manipulated and their positions changed by the dealer,[8] so it is almost impossible to win. To participate in the game, everybody has to de-

---

[6]"Momenti mori" is a Latin phrase meaning "Remember that you must die." The Christian era added "et resurrectionis," meaning "and resurrection," as a promise of new life.—Translator

[7]An "imbroglio" is a swindle or con trick.

[8]Note that the swindle involves both the player who is the dealer and an *accomplice* who pretends to be an ordinary participant, but who is actually raising the stakes of the bets.

fine his or her role, make a selection, and bet on one of the three possibilities as to what Dino is, then winning or losing his or her bet. Everybody plays and enjoys him- or herself with cathartic laughter all around, betting mostly on "Dino is lazy."

By limiting the probabilities and amplifying the theme of the "imbroglio" and complicity, the game of three cards is a metaphorical prelude to the larger problems of choice and of definition. The game returns to Dino his "card" of adolescence and gives the family a less symbiotic environment by differentiating each member of the family while playing.

THE CONSULTATION WITH CARL WHITAKER

In the course of the eleventh session the therapist declares that he needs help "because I'm getting too close to this apron with so many children attached . . . I'm at risk of getting entangled myself!" He presents the family with the possibility of a consultation with "a professor from America," and the consultation with Dr. Carl Whitaker is received with interest by the family.

Mother: (starts to talk with euphoria) Did you hear? We're going to America (*as if it were about an official voyage to a distant continent*).

Dr. Whitaker intervenes, rarely looking the family in the face. The female translator seems to talk for him, since it is her voice that sounds calm and clear. Whitaker's hand is on Andolfi's shoulder. Soon the consultant becomes a co-therapist. The bond between the two therapists, the verbal and nonverbal contents of the transactions, and the presence of the translator enhance their emotional distance from the family and allow a higher level of meta-communication.

The central theme is the funeral of "mother as myth," the gravestone over her tomb, and whether there will be a single grave or ossuary for the whole family. To celebrate the ritual

of mother's funeral there are several conditions. The first is
that Gino, who has not joined the sessions for the third time
in a row, is to be seen as the person that the family has chosen not to change. His absences, in contrast to Dino's, are
a message about maintaining the static nature of the myth.
Gino's absence is a mirror of the internal and apparently im-
mutable image of reciprocal union, harmony, and happiness,
which contrasts with the helpful message provided by Dino,
who was present even when he was absent.

Whitaker: If the family changes, this can be painful for everybody. Maybe that's exactly what Gino is trying to do, to
stop this from happening, because if he has been acting
as a mother since the death of father, trying to avoid the
children's suffering, that means that he acted like a
mother (*according to an implicit stereotype of the overprotec-
tive mother hen who stunts growth*).

Therapist: (to Whitaker) So you're saying that today we have
seven children here and that the mother isn't here.

Whitaker: Yes, because when the father died Mama became
Papa, I mean, *a hero*. In these cases what happens is that
the oldest child becomes the mother (*in a sacrificing role*).

Therapist: I'm not sure if you are saying that the mother has
become the father of the family or if the mother has become the oldest child in the family.

Whitaker: I don't know, since I don't know this family well
enough to say. What usually happens (*here Whitaker uses
his own experience as a much older person than the therapist*) is
that when the father dies, the mother takes his place and
becomes father and somehow the family elects some-
body to substitute for the mother and become the new
mother. In this family I believe that it's the oldest son,
Gino, who chooses to substitute himself to be a sacrificing mother. Therefore, by not participating in the sessions, he has chosen to become a "nobody" for three
sessions so that other people wouldn't suffer. (*Sym-*

bolically "nobody" indicates the void his useless sacrifice does not fill.)

Mario: I'm the second son and I can say that maybe all this happened, but not on account of Gino. The one who directed the family was my brother Dino. Gino is the selfish type, the type who takes what he can and doesn't concern himself with giving. He was always like that. (*The value of the symptom and Dino's centrality are declared explicitly in this last phase of the therapeutic process.*)

Whitaker: Maybe today there could be a new election. We could elect a new mother; as a result the old Mama who became Papa isn't needed. She could simply be a person, instead of being a father . . . for example, becoming more selfish, not in the sense of stealing from other people, but in the sense of turning her shoulders away from everyone except herself.

Therapist: I believe that you have a whole support system around you that helps you to stay a heroine.

Dino: Practically speaking, is this a bad situation?

Whitaker: It's probably hopeless. (*Homeostatic feedback by Whitaker about the shifts in perceptual differentiation enacted.*)

Therapist: The risk for me is to become a hero in a family of heroes. And therefore to fail myself as well.

Whitaker: I would worry about that. Or they could drive you crazy!

Therapist: (*smiling*) This seems better to me!

Whitaker: Because you could have fun?

Therapist: Yes.

Whitaker: You could then become Mama's favorite.

Therapist: But then Dino would kill me. Dino would never put up with my stealing his mama. Once we fantasized about his mama, for example, that she would remarry. Dino was extremely angry, I've never seen such a strong reaction. He would have killed that man and maybe even his mother!

Whitaker: If she dies, we could give her a beautiful funeral . . . and I would cry for so long. I think there could be a beautiful grave . . . with a gravestone above. I was thinking what we could write on the stone (*raising his hands, accompanying with a gesture his fantasy*): "Here lies the most marvelous mother in the world." I would write it in my handwriting. We could invite all these people (*pointing to various family members*) to this funeral.

Mother: (*increasingly tense*) Excuse me, Professor, we didn't come here for my funeral, we're here because of Dino's strange ways. (*The more the tension increases, the more her distress shifts. She immediately reaches for Dino as a protective screen.*)

Therapist: I think that Dino has the crazy idea that he's sexy (*amplifying her distress*).

Whitaker: Maybe this keeps Mama young. I just had this crazy thought. Probably Dino is like Ulysses: he travels away but always returns to his bride. What was she called?

Caterina and Elena: Penelope.

The dream of eternal love recurs in literature, like Homer's masterpiece, *The Odyssey*, and the Faustian myth of eternal youth. In order for Lucia, the mother, to be seen as a person, even her attachment to Dino, vital and exciting to both of them, must be seen in a realistic time frame, contrasting her older age and eventual death with his youth, as emphasized by Whitaker's fantasy of the grave.

Whitaker: Yes, yes . . . and you (*turning to Dino*), what would you write on your mother's grave?

Dino: Uh, nothing.

Whitaker: That wouldn't be nice. And you, ma'am, what would you write on your gravestone?

Mother: (*confusing herself with Dino*) "My sorrowful mother."

Dino: (*laughs*)

Therapist: I don't believe that mother could stand to be alone in a tomb. If she really decided to die, I think that she would have to go into a large ossuary where everybody's bones are and where you don't know what belongs to whom.

Whitaker: Do you think that all the children would like to be buried there with her?

Therapist: I don't know. Maybe some of them would prefer to be placed in a common tomb and wish that there would be someone capable of personally identifying them. I don't know where the father is. Do you think that there is an inscription on his tomb?

Whitaker: "A dead hero."

Therapist: "Pray for me and do not grow."

In the interactive sequences presented above, through a highly provocative interchange with a rapid composition and fading of images, based on a continual and unpredictable shift of symbols, the precarious existential state of the family is made explicit in an almost epigrammatic way, suspended as they are between history and myth. The greater the dead heroes, the greater the misery of the living.

For the first time, Dino's "foolish" behavior is redefined by Whitaker as "impertinent," through his use of the absurd,[9] because if it is true that Dino is the one who dictates the rules, it is also true that he does not yield to the rules of the others, in this way creating disorder. But his play is pointless, like Gino's absence and mother's useless sacrifices, as it kills

---

[9]In Latin *absurdus* literally means "that cannot be heard." According to the existentialists, the condition of man after the Second World War is absurd. Without metaphysical faith, man finds himself exiled in a world without meaning because it has neither harmony nor order. The term "absurd," used in the sense of "dissonant," indicates any judgment or proposition contrary to the rules of a given system of inferences. Referring to Whitaker specifically and his systematic use of the absurd in therapy, see Whitaker (1975, 1984).

the living and magnifies the heroes who are only a constella-
tion of ghosts of the mind.

THE GLOBE AND THE DIVISION OF LANDS

Four months after the consultation with Carl Whitaker and 13
months after the beginning of therapy, it is Dino who speaks
out providing evidence of the changes that have occurred.

Dino: I have understood one thing, that it's necessary to go
    and knock someone off their pedestal . . .
Gino: Excuse me, Dino, I've got to say something. Even if I
    wasn't present at the last session, at home we talked a
    lot about what happened with Dr. Andolfi and Professor
    Whitaker. You don't remember much about Papa, but I
    remember a lot. Papa walked up and down the corridor,
    forward and backward, day and night, because he didn't
    succeed in bringing up the family as he wanted to. He
    fathered us, but he did it with Mama, they are both re-
    sponsible, "50–50." We were badly conceived and badly
    raised. Mama got together with Papa who was very un-
    balanced and, with her prickly personality, she only con-
    tinued to unbalance this family. And we paid for it.
    However, if someone continually says all his life that he's
    unbalanced, not understanding, always blaming his par-
    ents, it will never end. We'll never stop, do you under-
    stand? If, instead, and I'm including myself, we get our
    bearings, we try to understand and accept Mama with
    her difficult temper, but we also try to understand Papa,
    then we'll begin to end it all. (*to Dino*) You, for example,
    did you ever ask yourself why you're like that? Why are
    you in the house from morning to night? Why don't you
    want to enjoy life, do something useful?
Dino: Yes, I've asked myself. But the problem is, it's not a
    problem that can be solved here. It's not a problem that
    can be solved with Dr. Andolfi.

Gino: We have to solve it ourselves.

Dino: It's a problem that we must solve ourselves, knocking down the pedestals. I don't know if you understand me, I don't know if I'm being clear.

Gino: (thoughtful) I want to understand better.

Dino: You, for example, you've got problems that you're not able to solve. My question is: Are you unable to solve them because you can't make it or because there's something behind you, someone who's holding you back?

Gino: (He watches Dino silently.)

Dino: If it's someone who's holding you back, we can't solve it by turning our backs away and just looking ahead.

Gino: Dino, after Papa, I was the first to fail, understand? The first child and the first brother.

Previously in therapy, it had been revealed that as a teenager Gino had been jailed for a short time for theft. He had struggled to regain his self-esteem as a responsible person ever since.

Dino: Wait a minute. *(turning to the therapist)* Dr. Andolfi, we've known each other for more than a year. What have you found out about our problems? What are your conclusions?

Therapist: Would you like an answer from me?

Dino: Yes.

Therapist: I found the syndrome of Atlas.

Dino: What does it mean?

Therapist: I found . . . the Atlas complex. Atlas was the one who carried the world on his shoulders.[10] This is the most important thing I've found.

---

[10]The Greek legend relates that the giant Atlas was condemned by Zeus for having helped the Titans, the children of Ouranos (the personification of Heaven) and Gaea (the personification of Earth), of immense stature and strength themselves, against the growing race of the gods of Olympus. For his unjust interference in the affairs between Heaven and Earth, the powerful giant Atlas was crushed forever by the weight of the world and his freedom was constrained by his burden of superhuman responsibility.

Mario: And who is Atlas?

Therapist: Atlas is the one who is called crazy.

Elena: Can you explain it better?

Mother: In clearer words?

Therapist: Do you all know who Atlas was?

Dino: No.

Caterina: I don't know. It seems to me Atlas was a mythological figure.

Therapist: That's right, a half-god.

Elena: Yes.

Therapist: He was an extraterrestrial . . . I don't know how to explain it. He wasn't a human being. Human beings who want to carry the world on their shoulders are called crazy. But the ones who make them carry it are also considered crazy, because everybody takes the piece of earth that belongs to them and loads it up on the shoulders of Atlas. And if Atlas continues to hold them up on himself, he is stupid. Understand, Dino? (*He gets up and writes "STUPID" on a blackboard.*)

Mario: Understand now, Dino?

Elena: Dino hasn't understood.

Dino: I didn't understand it very well, because I think our problems are difficult to solve, doctor.

Therapist: Do you want to know why it's difficult? Because no one in this family remembers Atlas.

Gino: We came here for you, OK? (*looks at Dino*).

Dino: (*raising his head with determination*) For me? And for what reason?

Gino: Because someone in the family thinks that you're crazy, that you're sick.

Dino: And what do you mean sick? Let's be serious, eh? Let's wake up! Because this story is getting serious. Let's be serious, because each of us here is talking without understanding. When you, Gino, speak for each of us it's difficult to understand, because each of us gets "disturbed" by certain situations.

Gino: (conciliatory) Dino, listen . . .

Dino: (agitated) No, you listen to me. Now we have to figure out if each of us gets lost in the crowd, or if we hide ourselves, or if we don't want to speak out, because for me to talk I have to knock some people off their pedestals and I can't do it, understand?

Mother: But you have to do it here.

Dino: (continuing his argument intensely) . . . Because at home, doctor, we don't talk together and they don't do anything but look at me and say, "You're sick. We're taking you to Rome." I even talked about not coming to Rome. I see it as a useless trip. It's more than a year . . . what do you think?

Therapist: I think that it's useless, too, if things don't change in Palermo, but tell me something . . .

Dino: I'll be happy to solve at least part of the problem. I'll be happy, then I'll sit down and put my soul to rest.

Therapist: The problem is to ask ourselves if there are lands that you want to return. That is, if you want to give back some continents, some oceans, some mountains.

Mario: Or whether you want to keep everything on top of you.

Gino: It's a big load.

Lucio: A load for each of us.

Dino: I'd like to settle this business and stop coming here to Rome.

Therapist: We need a map of the world or a globe.[11]

Dino: A globe?

---

[11]Soon the group of observers behind the mirror get a large globe from a nearby stationery shop and give it to the therapist, in order to make the image of Atlas and the world that he carries on his shoulders concrete and tangible.

Mother: A globe, like the one we have at home.

Dino: . . . Well, because I've noticed that each of us is disturbed. Either we end this story or we don't. I've realized that I'm fed up having people behind me. I want to be at peace for a while. Because I—I never said anything to the rest of you, but I'm tormented 24 hours a day.

First Whitaker and now Dino offers the therapist the chance to let the gods step down from the pedestal. This requires debunking spurious family myths (for example, father as the quintessence of all virtues) and decoding ambiguous family rules (for example, the rule that women are successful, men are failures). This will shed light on Dino's "humanitarian problem of abstract and concrete organs" from the second session, and his imaginary illnesses and real voids.

Responding to Dino's questions with a mythological image, the therapist wants to stress the circular character of the family pathology that he now defines as an idealization, serving to keep the myth in place from generation to generation. This imprint of needs existed before the birth of Dino.

It is crazy for Dino, as it was for the mythological Atlas, to interfere in disputes that are not his own and have their own history, in the vain hope of healing what is out of his control. Specifically, Dino has given up his own growth to identify with someone whose function is to keep in place and weld together into the family myth the cultural, social, and ethnic stereotypes of his predecessors. These stereotypes are the "reparative expectations" for humiliations suffered. Two examples are the paternal grandmother, who was considered a failure because she had no children for 15 years, and the maternal grandmother, who was betrayed and abandoned by her unfaithful husband. As another example of "invisible loyalties" (Boszormenyi-Nagy, 1987; Boszormenyi-Nagy & Spark, 1973), we see Lucia as someone who was married too young to a partner who she was not convinced was right for her, in order to shield the shame of her father who abandoned the family, and who sacrificed herself in the exemplary role of Mother (with a capital M). Or else we see Giovanni as an only child who had to have many children whom he could not support, in order to fulfill his own father's wish (who was also an only child) to have a large family.

To take charge of all the family failures is not only unreasonable, it is foolish, since no one now remembers who made the sacrifice or the reparative expectations for which it was made. To recapture the meaning and the value of time in the therapeutic context, as a learning arena, it is useful to use a real globe. This will serve as an intermediate object between real responsibilities and the still cloudy perception of the delegate functions guaranteed by each member of the family. The reciprocity of the process of escaping the world, by which each person avoids facing his own responsibility, is stressed when the therapist asks Dino if he is ready to give back to the others the lands that belong to them. The commitment to choose in this case is defined as reciprocal. The others can reappropriate the lands unfairly given to the patient only to the extent that Dino himself is prepared to return them. Confronted with the choice and provoked out of his stupidity by the therapist's words, Dino no longer chooses to take refuge behind the shield of his "don't know's" and the mask of a fool. Dino can now express his own suffering, which echoes Gino's suffering. Gino expresses his desperation, making himself a spokesman of the desperation of his mother and of his siblings.

Gino: Even Mama is desperate for me, for Mario, for Livio. She's desperate for Andrea, for Lucio, for Caterina, for Elena and for herself.

Lucia is seen in the end here, even by the son who still antagonizes her, as an individual, and as a woman with feelings. This change of context allows the therapist to widen the breach already opened by Gino, devoting for the rest of the session special attention to the three women in the family: mother, Elena, and Caterina. Facing Dino, he says, "Atlas here is at rest," and he assumes the weight and takes charge of therapy to make a more difficult step. He directly confronts the women on the level of their interpersonal failures, freeing them from the unreasonable societal assumption that women, by definition, have to be strong.

Therapist: (turning initially towards Gino) Gino, what territories did you put on Dino's shoulders that Dino still holds, thinking he is a god? *(silence)*

Gino: My insecurity. Yes, my fear of being a mixed-up person.

Therapist: (turning to Elena) Elena, which of your territories does that nut Atlas pretend to carry on his shoulders?

Elena: (being evasive) I don't know, you should ask him.

Therapist: It doesn't matter. You look a lot like Mama, Elena.

Elena: Could be.

Therapist: Maybe I've never succeeded in reaching you in these sessions, to get at something of yours, just as I didn't succeed in reaching Mama. And yet, if you recognized and accepted something of your own, maybe Mama would be less of a "monster."

Mario: Elena is a level-headed woman, doctor.

Therapist: (pushing the globe to Elena) A territory doesn't necessarily have to be an ugly territory. It could be an important territory, even beautiful or in bloom, but always a territory that ends up on the shoulders of Atlas. *(Elena says she does not understand, displaying the avoidance mechanism described above.)*

Therapist: (turning to the mother) Since the two of you look so much alike, maybe you'll be able to squeeze out of Elena what she can't pull out of herself. We're not looking for the guilty one, for goodness sake! We want to see if this nut Atlas can finally retire and be an adolescent. That's the goal. If he's reborn an adolescent, adults must also be reborn to take responsibility for their own lands. Each of them can take, for example, a piece of South America, a piece of the Pacific Ocean, a piece of Europe, and so on. Otherwise crazy Atlas won't budge.

Elena: If only I knew, if only I understood . . .

Mother: Maybe Dino thinks that if he had been older, if it had been him in his father's place, all that took place between me and Elena wouldn't have happened.

Dino: What do you mean "if he had been older"?

Mother: You were little then, you were 12 years old. And Elena was 20. Like me when I got married. I fought with my daughter. I didn't want her to leave the house so soon.

Lucio: And my sister left home.

Mother: I was afraid for her—that she would make mistakes. And I was afraid for me—because I needed her, her calm, her affection.

Elena: Don't exaggerate, Mama.

Therapist: Listen to your mama. It's the first time that she doesn't look like a "monster" to keep at bay.

Elena: Maybe my mother resented the fact that I left, but I'm not sure.

Mother: (*moved*) I felt her absence. (*turning to her daughter*) I felt your absence so much. I felt abandoned. (*silence*)

Therapist: (*taking the globe between his hands and placing one hand on the mother's shoulder and the other on Elena's, sitting beside her*) Which lands can you take back here?

Elena: OK, I'll tell you right now what I dumped on the shoulders of Atlas: my emptiness.

Lucio: We all missed Elena so much.

Dino: Sorry, what does "emptiness" mean?

Therapist: Not taking care of you as your sister, or as a stepmother, or like the one who maintains the image of Papa as a great man.

Elena: Maybe the third hypothesis is more true, because I always tried to understand, like Papa did.

Therapist: (*again indicating the globe*) When you find your continent we'll put a cross on it. It's yours.

Elena: (turning the globe and pointing decisively) This one, Africa, right here.

Therapist: Africa belongs to you and to Papa. After all, it's a very large continent, which can be shared. *(turning now to Caterina)* And you, Caterina? Which territory of yours did you put on Atlas's shoulders? *(smiling)* Africa is already taken by Elena and Papa.

Caterina: By talking, we understand each other better. Today Mama helped Elena. It's the first time I heard Mama different in many years. As for me, I don't know. Me and Dino were very close when we were children. We talked, we gossiped, we discussed, we played, we went out together. Until this drug business happened, then there was a clean break.

Mario: It was an abandonment.

Elena: Abandonment. Exactly.

Dino: (defensively) Sorry, instead of abandonment couldn't it be that I took another road?

Caterina: Sure. But I suffered. I even suffered because I didn't know how to get close to you.

Therapist: And what's left burdening the shoulders of Dino-Atlas?

Caterina: The lack of a girlfriend to confide in and to talk openly with. All right, then, I'll choose the United States.

Mother: Dino felt abandoned.

Dino: You're still talking about me? Listen, doctor, I want my part too . . . for myself I want California. California is my chunk of responsibility in this family.

Therapist: You wait, because if you don't give everything back first, you can't choose anything for yourself. And Mama?

Mother: I was wrong too, I was wrong because I didn't give my son Dino the necessary assistance. It started before the death of my husband, it continued with the money which was never enough, and ended with Elena leaving home. I'll take Saudi Arabia.

Selecting a very powerful territory, but also the most intricate one, as it is linked to economic interests, the mother reappropriates the responsibility she had delegated to the others. She takes back the care of Dino, her most vulnerable child, who is stuck in the middle between the older ones and the younger ones. This gap in maternal care was not filled by anybody else. Even Lucio, with his good intentions, was unable to supply this caring and ended up making Dino feel unbalanced—sometimes older, sometimes much younger and always fragile. The fear of separation, understood as abandonment, is drawn clearly in this session. The goal to achieve in shattering the myth of Atlas is to take back one's own territory, while remaining a group.

The two opposing processes of amplification and metonymy are the therapeutic ingredients used in this session. Amplification is the process of enlarging the context (Andolfi et al., 1983), while metonymy is a restricting process, where parts stand for wholes. For those directly involved, the task is to discover the right dimension of things.

Therapist: Today, for the first time, I feel I have located the lands of the women in the family. May I ask you something? At home, using your globe I want each of you to repeat this game, committing yourselves to retaking the territory to which you are entitled! I ask you, however, not to take the world away from the shoulders of Atlas until you've shown the will to reclaim the lands that belong to you.

Dino: What the hell is this about lands? I have my problems too!

Therapist: I'm sorry that you're suffering, Dino.

Dino: (decisively) Do what you want, let's stop here!

Elena: (laughing and hugging her brother) He's great!

Dino: Now, for sure, I don't like Atlas anymore.

Dino's salvation and his capacity for self-determination lies in his refusal to continue to consider the legend of Atlas true for him and in not agreeing to perpetuate the analogy with the hero of the mythological fable. If Dino ceases to be a giant, the mother will not be able to continue to be a heroine, and nobody else will be able to play the part of the failure anymore or even just the winner in the family. This includes the father, who once again becomes part of everybody's feelings and awareness in a more tangible, human way.

Contrasting the myth of the father (in reality a half-man) with the myth of Atlas (a half-god), the therapist succeeds in meta-communicating about Dino's protective and super-human functions. Dino, in fact, believed he was able to act as a hinge. Using the myth of Atlas as a metaphor, the therapist succeeds in making the family see how even mythical time, initially believed to be ahistorical by the family, can finally be perceived in its developmental pattern, in sequences, allowing space for individual growth.

If the image of the dead father is recognized as unreal, the family can finally feel his physical absence and mourn his loss. Even the function of the giant Atlas enacted by Dino and interpreted through his psychotic behavior will be recognized as useless. This will make room for his needs as an adolescent who demands some real space to grow inside and outside the family.

GIFTS FOR THE GRANDCHILDREN

In the thirteenth session the family's arrival with boxes of gifts for an upcoming holiday offers the therapist the cue for opening up a new dimension. This is the fourth generation, which reinvigorates the resources of the family through a generational shift. The exploration moves in this way from a relationship between the ever-present mama and her ever-dependent children to that between grandmother and grandchildren.

Therapist: (turning to Mrs. Penna, who has a colored package in her arms) And what's this?

Mother: Big Jim! (*with pride*). It's a gift for my grandchild, Marco.

Therapist: It's the first time I see you as a grandmother!

Mother: As a matter of fact, I raised Marco along with Caterina and Elena. He comes to see me, he phones me. Sometimes I have to say to my daughter Elena, in spite of my love for her, "Elena, don't be so hard on the child!"

Elena: I'm his mother, understand. I have to raise him, together with my husband.

Mother: All right, but don't punish him too often. You're too strict. He's a child, he has to play, you have to understand that.

Therapist: Good, good. If everybody can have a family and make it their "own," maybe Atlas will really be able to retire and Lucia can play at being a grandmother, finally!

Gino: But my children don't feel the need for a grandmother.

Therapist: You are the father. They feel as much "need" for a grandmother as you allow them to feel. Don't you trust her as a grandmother?

Gino: No, because she never loved my children.

Therapist: (*to Gino*) Do you play with your children? And do you think they wouldn't enjoy themselves with their grandmother?

Gino: Of course I play with them, and how! At mealtimes I'm between my two daughters. On my right there's my wife, and in front of me there's my little boy, Giovanni. At dinner, I joke around a lot, I talk to them, we tell stories, we fool around together. I'm a real comedian! At home we hug each other, we dance, my little boy too. . . . But, when it's necessary, I know how to scold them too. Before, we used to go to the country, to our beautiful cottage. Not now. Because on Sunday, when I go with my children, my mother wants us to tidy up the place and put everything in order. And my children won't do that because they want to play in the country, and she tells them off because they make a mess.

Mario: The fact is that when we go to the country, we like to go and rest. We take our stuff, the food already pre-pared, because we want to relax and not to be bothered with our daily hassles, not to be bossed around by some-body. My wife doesn't like to be ordered around either. And now, she's pregnant again. Carla, my wife, wants to go to the country, but she feels uncomfortable there.

Elena: Your wife is wrong, because this problem doesn't exist.

Caterina: Nobody wants to order anybody around. You go to the country to have a pleasant day.

Therapist: It's incredible! We start with the children and we always end up with the adults! What do the children do?

Gino, Elena, and Mario: (laughing) They run around and have the best time in the world.

Therapist: (to Dino) Who do you think will have children, after those of you who already have them?

Dino: I wouldn't know.

Therapist: (to Lucio) Do you see yourself as a father?

Lucio: I'm engaged to a great girl, but I still don't see myself as a father.

Dino: I feel really incapable. The idea of a child scares me, because I don't feel up to it. I mean, I wouldn't know what to teach them.

Gino: (laughing) Don't bring up the same old story that you're always the problem, eh?!

Therapist: (smiling) Still, I would like to see you with children! Maybe you would discover that grandmother is very good with grandchildren and that you can trust her . . .

Mother: And who pays for the train tickets?[12]

Elena: Everybody pays for themselves and for their own children!

---

[12]During the course of therapy, a recurrent problem was that the children were completely dependent on the mother, even for their travel expenses to get to Rome.

Gino: Given my financial situation, it's difficult for me.

Therapist: After all, we'll see you again in six to eight months. You'll have time to plan and put aside some money.

Mario: My child is two years old. And in six months we'll be taking care of a newborn.

Therapist: All right, it's not necessary that you all come together. Whoever can come will come.

Elena: I willingly bring my son. Of course, Rome is a big city, and he could get lost. I take the risk anyway.

Therapist: Then it's not too soon to talk about the risks of living. I was afraid there was too much death around.

Gino: I'm just about to start a new life. Maybe it's thanks to Giovanni the Evangelist; didn't he predict the resurrection in the Gospel? (*He laughs, and the others, including Dino, laugh too.*)

Therapist: (*to the mother*) But your children, especially the boys, think that you are an untouchable grandmother, without even a little tenderness.

Mother: I'm not interested in what they think, I stay at my own house. When my daughter comes, she brings her child. If she asks me if she can leave him, I say yes and he's happy.

Therapist: And you, are you happy?

Mother: Yes, yes, very happy.

Elena: Marco is an affectionate child, very sociable, he isn't shy.

Mother: I am frank, I tell it like it is. But I love my grandchildren and they know I do. If anything, it's my own children who don't find me sincere.

Therapist: (*to Elena*) And do you trust her?

Elena: In what sense?

Therapist: That grandmother isn't an old witch, but a good grandmother.

Elena: I trust her.

Gino: I don't trust her.

Mario: I think grandparents always want to limit children, not to let them go. I'm always telling my mother: if Francesco, my son, doesn't want to come to you, don't insist, maybe he isn't ready just then.

Mother: I'm not the type to insist . . .

Mario: I tell her so she will understand. Children need to be respected.

Therapist: In short, you trust her only halfway?

Mario: Let me explain better, doctor. I don't want Francesco to feel distant from my mother, from his aunts and uncles and certainly not from us, his parents. On the contrary I really want him to feel close to everybody.

Therapist: But you're still not convinced. Maybe because here we have a grandmother who still does not feel accepted at all as a grandmother. What happened to the doll? The one I gave you months ago, that Dino tried to destroy, throwing it in a trash can?[13]

Mother: Dino was jealous of the doll, so I keep it locked up in a cupboard. That reminds me, we always leave the doll behind in Palermo.

Therapist: Keep it, Signora, until you can bring it back. It's like a pledge between us. (*looking at everybody*) The effort that I want to ask you to make is to allow grandmother to spend a lot of time with her grandchildren, until we see each other again. What I mean is, she has to spend time with each of her grandchildren individually and not just with her favorite, Marco, to get to know each of them better and let them get to know her better too. You can all help your mother and the grandchildren by express-ing interest and pleasure when your children go to see grandmother Lucia.

---

[13]This refers to an episode that the family discussed in the tenth session. The therapist offered a cloth doll to the mother, declaring his confidence that, in spite of all her faults, Lucia could prove herself capable of tender-ness, playing with it and having experiences as a grandmother with her grandchildren.

Gino: Who knows if my mother, with these children who run around her, will start being a grandmother and who knows if Dino, seeing his mother play with the grand-children, will be able to cut the cord? That doll that you gave to my mother months ago, do you know that he would have torn it apart then?

Therapist: We can make an appointment with the children in six months. (*warmly*) Dino didn't talk much. Let's hope that he won't transform himself from Atlas to Herod![14] (*Everybody laughs.*)

Mother: Then we'll see you again in six months. We'll go get an appointment with the secretary. And after?

Therapist: In three or four years.

THE FOLLOW-UP

A year after the last session, the therapist has a telephone conversation with the mother in Palermo. Mrs. Penna says she is happy that he called and that she has not forgotten her promise to return to Rome with her grandchildren. She adds that the family is still not ready, "because not all my children can afford to pay for the tickets for themselves and for their own families from their own pockets." This has now become a necessary condition, since she decided, "I don't want to be the bank anymore."

The news the mother gives about the family's improvement in the year's interval since the last session is, as she herself says, "80% satisfactory." Dino has had no more psychotic ep-isodes and hospital admissions. "He no longer takes drugs" and no longer has any symptoms of a fugue state with police involvement. However, he still lives at home and "sleeps in late in the morning." Lucio has found work as a business consultant and is thinking of getting married as soon as his

---

[14]Herod, King of Judea in the time of Jesus, ordered the destruction of infants in Bethlehem, which provoked the flight of Jesus, Mary, and Joseph into Egypt.—Translator

finances will allow it ("to bring home a stable salary"); Livio
and Andrea have finished high school. Livio has already
started working as a radio technician and Andrea is looking
for work, even if "it isn't easy to find a job these days." Caterina teaches in junior high school, is expecting her first
child, and is very happy. Her husband, who works at a bank,
is a fine person. She often sees Elena, her husband, and their
son, Marco. Gino has his ups and downs. Sometimes "he's
warm to me and sometimes he accuses me." The mother still
feels that he has not found the right road and that he "should
do more for his own children." All her grandchildren visit
her and she enjoys playing cards with them, preparing nice
meals for them, and receiving them lovingly in the country
with eggs fresh from the hen.

The telephone call concludes with the mother saying she
referred to the Institute a family among her in-laws who
"have psychological problems with their daughter."

Mother: I have faith in you, Dr. Andolfi. I hope we'll be able to
    have more faith in ourselves. We are still not sure
    enough to trust each other. We'll see you again as soon
    as possible.

Two Years Later

The family referred by the Pennas has made contact with the
Institute and started therapy. In the meantime, Gino called
the therapist twice to say that "things are getting better."
Again, it is Dr. Andolfi who telephones. This time he speaks
first to Dino then to his mother.

Dino states that he is looking for a permanent job. Andrea
has settled down with a skilled job in a company, but Dino is
worried for himself. He does not know when he will find a
good job.

Dino: Yes, I get some little jobs, here and there, not much, as
    a handyman or electrician.

Therapist: And at home?

Dino: We're still here, but we had the house redone: it's a little more modern now. As for moving, it's out of the question.

Therapist: And what do you do, when you're not working? Do you go to soccer games?

Dino: No, I don't follow soccer much.

Therapist: Do you do anything?

Dino: Really, I try to understand better, inside of me. And I listen to music.

Therapist: Modern music or classical?

Dino: Modern.

Therapist: Do you have a stereo?

Dino: I have a good tape recorder and sometimes I listen to it with a friend.

Therapist: Did you ever think of calling in the past two years?

Dino: Telephoning? No. I thought of meeting you. I would like to take a trip.

Therapist: Would you come alone? Or do you still doubt that the family can get on alone, without you? Especially your mama! Do you remember two years ago, when we last met, what we talked about?

Dino: Yes, I remember talking about relationships between brothers and sisters and about little children.

Therapist: Was anyone else born in the meantime?

Dino: Yes, Caterina's daughter. I would like to have a child too, but I'm not ready. Maybe one day. . . . Well, we'll see you, doctor. I'll pass you on to mama. She came in and she's right beside me.

The mother teases Dr. Andolfi that she heard he had been in Sicily for a conference and did not go to visit them.

Mother: Doctor, I'm very pleased to hear from you again, but I would have been happier to see you in Palermo. Why didn't you come to visit us? It would have been a lovely surprise. We are well, and you? Yes, Lucio got married, he's happy; me too. Dino is still at home, but he hasn't had any more crises. One thing I know now is that my children, especially the boys, all take a little more time, but they make it, doctor, between the highs and the lows. But you must promise to come and visit, here at home. You want to know if our house is still a sanctuary? (*The therapist is referring to the session about their dining room having become the father's shrine.*) No, it's no longer a sanctuary. Come in person and see for yourself. We're expecting you.

Dr. Andolfi assures her that he will keep his promise.

Glossary

NOTE: *Terms that appear in italics in the definitions are defined elsewhere in this glossary.*

Actions in Therapy: behaviors that are prescribed by the therapist to the family, in or out of the session, and that serve to dramatize daily events of family life, moods, relationships among various family members, and so on, in the form of representative actions, such as rituals and sculpting. The passage from words to actions, which can also utilize suitable objects to create a particular context, often works to produce a perceptual change in how each person sees situations, behaviors, and relationships. "Enacting" in therapy can therefore produce greater effects than talking, bypassing daily defensive habits and bringing long-repressed emotions to light.

Context Markers: correspond to individual acts or behaviors (verbal or nonverbal), images, objects, environmental or individual characteristics, rituals, and communicative redundancies (patterns) that are especially meaningful and "signal" a specific context, contributing to defining it or maintaining it. Recognizing context markers, therefore, cannot be separated from an analysis of the "meaning" attributed to the elements that constitute it by those who participate in the interaction. It is only the attribution of meaning, in fact, that permits the transformation of individual "contents" or "implications" of a message into the context markers of the message.

Embarrassment: conveys a sense of awkwardness, bewilderment, and perplexity. We choose the term *embarrassment* because it grasps the sense of personal fragility and insecurity and it sweeps away any possible confusion with the concept of blame, which provokes and amplifies the individual's defenses.

Family Myth: a filter for "reading" reality (in which both real and fantasy elements coexist)—partly "inherited" from the family of origin, partly constructed by the current family according to its emotional needs—that assigns each family member a well-defined role and script. The family myth interacts with personal myths of individual family members, shaping them and becoming shaped by them. Specific events of their individual or family life, especially during critical periods (such as births, deaths, weddings, personal milestones), determine which elements or roles of the mythical plot become activated in the form of particular "mythical constellations" stimulated by the specific situation.

Family Rituals: a series of actions and behaviors, coded strictly within the family, that repeat themselves over time and in which some or all of the members participate. They have the task of transmitting to the participants particular values, attitudes, or ways of behaving in specific situations, or emotional experiences bound to them. At the same time, however, they lend themselves to support the meanings that each member attributes to them, becoming enriched over time with new valences and thus providing a structure (like *context markers*) for the successive transformations of the *family myth*.

Humor in Therapy: a fundamental ingredient of relational play, it assures a kind of subtle continuity, a *context marker* capable of guaranteeing everyone the permission to continue to play with problems without feeling diminished or judged by doing it. Learning to smile, through a rediscovery of daily language and an attitude of optimism, at even serious difficulties and problems permits individuals to be seen as if "from the outside." This can occur to the degree that the people are involved "in it up to their necks." Together with *laughter in therapy*, humor is a powerful instrument through which to introduce empathy into therapeutic work. At the same time, if one succeeds in touching some of the relational rules of the family and to shift their level, one produces an increase in interpersonal tension in the session, which is indispensable for sparking a process of change.

Identified Patient as Ariadne's Thread: the patient is more than a portal of entry into the family system; he or she functions as a guide of the therapeutic process. In this function, the patient is a sort of Ariadne's thread to orient us in the labyrinth of the family system. The therapist must first be concerned with the identified patient as Ariadne's thread (the therapeutic process) before moving on to Ariadne herself (the patient as an individual).

Identified Patient as Regulator of the Therapeutic Process: a term referring to the guiding function played by the identified patient during therapy, in the search for rules and for sensitive areas of the family. With his behavior, the identified patient "signals" the variations in tension that occur (in the session or at home) within the family system; the therapist gathers this information, organizes it, and translates it for the family. From the *intensity*, persistence or variations in the signals, the therapist is able to calibrate the therapeutic relationship and the timing of his interventions. The function of "meaningful medium" given to the patient in considering him "the portal of entry into the family system" is thus extended throughout the whole course of therapy.

Imprint of Needs: a term to indicate how the unsatisfied needs of relationships with significant family members are stamped into each person. This makes the demand to satisfy these needs remain always in the present, continually seeking solutions in other relationships in order to compensate for the original "absence." These "stand-ins" will almost always be inadequate to satisfy the expectations placed on them due to their only partial similarity with the people who "ought" to satisfy them (for example, a partner cannot be the father or the brother who is sought).

Intensity: the strength of the urgency that the therapist's intervention creates when confronting the rules it counters, evoking in those involved corresponding emotional reactions or creating a context charged with tension. Intensity is maximal when a successful *therapeutic provocation* is made to the family or one of its members. This provocation is initially amplified by the therapist in order to increase its efficacy (compression phase), while he tries to "deflect" (decompression phase) the emotions aroused by the provocation in the family members with images and memories that evoke shared experiences.

Intimacy: corresponds to the moment of more closely approaching the family or one of its members by the therapist, who succeeds in grasping particular moods or relational problems to the degree that he is able to make them his own for a moment, identifying with the individuals who are living through them and sharing their problems with them. Such a moment takes place as part of a complex movement in which, after an approach phase, the therapist tries to move away again to reestablish the necessary space to search for a solution.

Joining: rather than a specific therapeutic technique, this term refers to an attitude that establishes an understanding with individual members of the family or with the whole family. Such an understanding can be achieved as the therapist succeeds in entering into contact with specific and emotionally relevant aspects of the "world" of the interlocutor, discovering the basis for each person's availability to get involved and to take personal risks for the change of relationships within the family.

Laughter in Therapy: has the function of "expelling" excess tension through channels of minor resistance. Laughter usually produces a sudden drop in resistance, an apparent moment of relaxation of the whole therapeutic system that allows itself a pause. The suspension of action that follows laughter produces a gap, a moment of silence, which allows a shift of emphasis from the interpersonal space—or the area of relationships—to an internal space, more undefended and vulnerable, in each individual.

Metaphor in Therapy: metaphoric images are considered here as central elements of verbal and nonverbal communication of the family and the therapist. The same symptomatic behavior can be understood as a relational metaphor, given the property of metaphor to convey many meanings (even contrasting ones) simultaneously, finding a mediating space for them in both the specificity and the generality of its contents. As the family members avail themselves of verbal metaphors, more or less consciously, to express their problems, or nonverbal metaphors to act them out, so the therapist uses them, fitting them creatively into his own metaphors, which he sends back to the family through verbal images, objects, or actions that suitably represent the family story.

Nodal Points: communicative redundancies (patterns), often nonverbal or paraverbal, usually ignored by the family, that lend themselves to the construction of a "relational map." These nodal points are grasped by the therapist, who uses them to punctuate in a different way both the relationships between the various participants and what happens in the session and to introduce new stimuli into the family's perceptual schema.

Playing in Therapy: represents the most articulated, the richest in nuances, the most personal means of engaging the family and the therapist in therapy. The "as if" of play creates a "psychological framework that permits one to discriminate between entities which belong to different logical types, that is, between messages composed of emotion-signs and messages composed of simulations of emotion-signs" (Valeri, 1979, p. 814). Playing in therapy transcends ludic (from the Latin "ludus," meaning play, game, or sport) activity in the strict sense and acquires a value in itself, a quality intrinsic to the therapeutic system. It helps the therapist and family members not to take themselves too seriously, to consider their own and others' definitions of reality as temporary and changeable, introducing flexibility and uncertainty into the therapeutic process. Playing can be an effective instrument to bind together the world of the adults, rich in abstract concepts and verbal communication, with the world of the children, in which nonverbal expression and concrete images predominate. The therapist can carry out a mediating action in this sense through *playing with objects* and *playing with words*.

Playing with Objects: a ludic (from the Latin "ludus," meaning play, game or sport) activity that uses material objects to represent behaviors, past or present relationships, and the rules of the family in treatment. The objects that the therapist introduces in the metaphoric play (see also *Metaphor in Therapy*) with the family acquire multiform characteristics because they simultaneously "are and are not" what they represent. They may be personal objects, taken from one of the family members, or objects introduced from the outside by the therapist (who can even offer himself as an "object" with whom to play); the choice depends on the circumstances, on the *therapeutic tempo,* and on the intensity of meaning attached to the object. Just as playing with objects can be useful to establish rapport and to create a crisis in the family, it is also a very effective way for the therapist to withdraw from the center of the therapeutic system. With the use of an object, he is no longer the reference point and the third side of new *relational triangles.* The focal point becomes the material object that is in the middle of the group, passed from one to the other, weighed and examined, as if it were a deep secret to be decoded.

Playing with Words: the construction of a metaphoric language (see *Metaphor in Therapy*) that originates from images that paint and sometimes camouflage or transform underlying moods, denied fears and conflicts, dysfunctional relational patterns, and so on. Such a language has a much longer and deeper period of permanence and cognitive resonance than a language based on abstract concepts or on verbal statements in the session. The curiosity sparked by the language of images, intentionally cryptic and incomplete, helps to tempt the individual and the whole family to participate in a therapeutic story belonging to all.

Prescriptive Strategy: the utilization of prescriptions, once or repeatedly, including ritualized forms (see *Therapeutic rituals*), to be worked out in the session or at home (in the intervals between sessions) to allow the emergence of important meanings and allegories that can confirm known schemata or to observe unforeseen aspects of emotional bonds among members of the family. We employ a prescriptive strategy to visualize the mythological system of the family and to allow it to develop (rather than to favor symptom remission) and to allow a possible change of the family rules.

Process of Separation: all the changes that bring the family and its individual members to develop a clearer identity, with an enlarging of space for autonomy for each individual and a redefinition of the content of the relational binds and the mutual expectations of the people who are involved. The process of separation occurs in a spatial dimension and a temporal one. The first refers to a space, identifiable in therapy with the *therapeutic space*, where each person's past experiences in their respective contexts are brought into the present. The second reflects the developmental time of the family, that is, the time needed to separate from old types of relationships in order to reconstruct them anew and to become aware of the changes. The *therapeutic tempo* has to enter the family's developmental time, pacing its process with the intervals between sessions and highlighting the changes that occur during the course of therapy.

Relational Networks: complex relational structures that obtain from the connections of the different *relational triangles* and that are modified by the variation of their configurations (see also *Trigenerational triangles*).

Relational Triangles: the elementary structures of all relationships, including those which apparently concern only two persons. Even in this case, in fact, it is possible to see how there exists, for each of the two people involved, a reference figure that acts as a third party in the relationship, even if he or she belongs to another space, to another time, or more frequently, to another generational level. With this, as with any other relational triangle, coalitions are possible, more or less masked, that produce dysfunctional relationships. The peculiarity is in the physical absence of one of the people of the triangle and the consequences arising from this.

Therapeutic Complicity: a stable understanding with the identified patient which becomes necessary when he or she recognizes his or her function as *regulator of the therapeutic process*. The more it is implicit and unverbalized, the more this complicity is useful and long-lasting, which places the patient in the special role of cotherapist. In order to analyze this understanding, it is necessary that the therapist is capable of (a) neutralizing early on the secondary gains that the patient tends to get from his or her position of being incapacitated or different, and (b) not interacting with only the negative identity that the identified patient presents.

Therapeutic Containment: an operation of support which must always accompany any provocative intervention in the therapist's interactions with the family and with each of the family members. Containment is indispensable for provocation to be therapeutic. The therapist must succeed in communicating that he is standing by the system while he is attacking it; that is, while he unmasks the rigidity of the family's behavioral and perceptual styles, he also understands the suffering bound to their emotional experiences and participates as a person who has had similar experiences. This is integrated with the opportunity that is given to each member of the family to open up his or her own problems and feelings without fear of disruptive consequences. The presence of the therapist and the therapeutic context guarantee a "container" for the emotions of the individuals and the family.

Therapeutic Provocation: a communicative modality, including an element of challenge, which aims to arouse areas of vulnerability in the patient or in another member of the family, and through him or her, of the whole family system. One tries in this way to stimulate in the person involved a reaction that permits the family to overcome relational problems with specific ways of behaving. It is essential to keep in mind that every therapeutic provocation, to be successful, must be accompanied by a concomitant action of *therapeutic containment* and of individual support.

Therapeutic Rituals: refer to a series of actions and repetitive behaviors of the whole therapeutic system or enacted by the family (or some of its members) at the explicit request of the therapist. In the first case, one identifies the actions and redundant behaviors in the therapist-family interactions that characterize each specific therapeutic context (the language of the therapist and the family, repetitive therapist-family interactions during the course of the session, "modeling" actions of the therapist and the family's response). In the second case, a ritual is constructed by the therapist that uses especially meaningful elements of the family's language and behavior by fitting them into prescriptions of behavior to be carried out in the session or beyond.

Therapeutic Script: the relational structure that involves family and therapist and that is constructed during the course of the therapeutic process, tending to substitute the script brought by the family when the family presents its own "drama." The therapist initially recognizes in the family script some *nodal points* of special emotional meaning for the people involved which he uses to propose an alternative "plot." From the integration of the two plots—the one proposed by the therapist and the one presented by the family—the therapeutic script originates, in a circular process of which the members of the therapeutic system (including the therapist) are only partially aware. This tends not only to restructure their relationships, changing the values of their contents, but also to reveal past gaps that went unnoticed, thus rediscovering the "missing" plot.

Therapeutic Space: the actual, concrete place where the sessions take place and where the therapist becomes the medium for the union of the diverse and far-flung contexts and experiences of each family member's story. These are thus brought into the present and placed into a larger framework, the "context of contexts," in which everyone tries to construct a new reality, separating oneself from the old one.

Therapeutic Story: in Italian, "storia" has several layers of meaning, including here both "story" as narrative and "history" as chronology. The therapist must first enter the family system and support the family story and then, from within this new configuration (the therapeutic system), construct a new therapeutic story. This requires the therapist to be an interacting member of the therapeutic system, allowing him to use his cognitive and emotional responses.

Therapeutic Tempo: in Italian, "tempo" has many layers of meaning, including those implied by "time" in English: period, phase, and season. In addition, it means "tempo" in the musical sense of rhythm, timing, or pace. There are diverse dimensions and aspects of time to consider in therapy. There is the therapeutic tempo in the narrow sense, referring to the timing or pacing of interventions, the moment when interventions should be made, taking into account the current context and the phase of the therapeutic process. More generally, the therapeutic tempo must enter the developmental time of the family: the time that is needed to elaborate the separation of old forms of relationships and construct them anew and to become aware of the changes. In this perspective, the temporal aspect of intervals between sessions paces the course of the therapeutic process and underlines the changes that occur in it.

Third Planet: a metaphoric image to indicate the therapeutic system which is produced by the encounter of two other "planets"—that of the family and that of the therapist. It represents the "space" in which the new system develops, paced by a tempo that follows the rhythm of the sessions and the evolution of the therapeutic process. The third planet therefore represents for both the family and the therapist a new space-time dimension, a territory that is neutral and without a history, through which to construct a different story that arises from the encounter.

Trigenerational Family: the extended family map obtained by using a spatial representation that ranges across a long vertical plane, crossed by at least three horizontal planes. All those who belong to the same generational level are placed on a horizontal plane, so that from high to low we find, respectively: the generation of the grandparents, that of the children and that of the grandchildren, united in various ways among themselves by *relational triangles* and *trigenerational triangles*, identified spatially by "family coordinates," which indicate the people involved and their level of belonging.

Trigenerational Triangles: those *relational triangles* in which the people involved find themselves located on three different generational levels (for example, grandfather–parent–grandchild).

Bibliography

Ackerman, N. W. Family psychotherapy: Theory and practice. *American Journal of Psychotherapy*, 1966, *3*, 409–414.

Ackerman, N. W. *Family Therapy in Transition.* Boston: Little, Brown, 1970a.

Ackerman, N. W. The art of family therapy In N. W. Ackerman (Ed.), *Family Therapy in Transition.* Boston: Little, Brown, 1970b.

Ackerman, N. W. Child participation in family therapy. *Family Process*, 1970c, *9* (4), 403–410.

Andolfi, M. *Family Therapy: An Interactional Approach* (Translated by H. R. Cassin). New York: Plenum Press, 1979.

Andolfi, M. Prescribing the families' own dysfunctional as a therapeutic strategy. *Journal of Marital and Family Therapy*, 1980, *6*, 29–36.

Andolfi, M., & Angelo, C. The therapist as director of the family drama. *Journal of Marital and Family Therapy*, 1981, *7* (3), 255–264.

Andolfi, M., & Angelo, C. Il sistema terapeutico ovvero il terzo pianeta. *Terapia Familiare*, 1984, *16*, 7–25.

Andolfi, M., & Angelo, C. Famiglia e individuo in una prospettiva trigenerazionale. *Terapia Familiare*, 1985a, *19*, 17–23.

Andolfi, M., & Angelo, C. Indicazioni e modalità di approccio in terapia familiare. *Psicologia Clinica*, 1985b, *2*, 265–278.

Andolfi, M., Angelo, C., Menghi, P., & Nicolò-Corigliano, A. M. *Behind the Family Mask: Therapeutic Change in Rigid Family Systems* (Translated by C. L. Chodorkoff). New York: Brunner/Mazel, 1983.

Andolfi, M., Cigoli, V., Loriedo, C., Nicolò-Corigliano, A. M., Pontalti, C., & Ugazio, V. Tavola rotonda su "Famiglia e individuo." In M. Andolfi & D. Piccone (Eds.), *La Formazione Relazionale. Individuo e Gruppo nel Processo di Apprendimento.* Rome: Institute of Family Therapy, 1985.

Andolfi, M., & Menghi, P. La prescrizione in terapia familiare: Parte prima. *Archivio di Psicologia, Neurologia e Psichiatria*, 1976, *4*, 434–456.

Andolfi, M., & Menghi, P. La prescrizione in terapia familiare: Il paradosso terapeutico. *Archivio di Psicologia, Neurologia e Psichiatria,* 1977, *1,* 57–76.

Andolfi, M., & Menghi, P. Provocative supervision. In J. Byng-Hall & R. M. Whiffen (Eds.), *Family Therapy Supervision.* New York: Academic Press, 1982.

Andolfi, M., Menghi, P., Nicolò, A. M., & Saccu, C. Interaction in rigid systems: A model of intervention in families with a schizophrenic member. In M. Andolfi & I. Zwerling (Eds.), *Dimensions of Family Therapy.* New York: Guilford Press, 1980.

Andolfi, M., & Piccone, D. (Eds.) *La Formazione Relazionale. Individuo e Gruppo nel Processo di Apprendimento.* Rome: Institute of Family Therapy, 1985.

Angelo, C. The use of the metaphoric object in family therapy. *American Journal of Family Therapy,* 1981, *9*(1), 69–78.

Anonymous. Toward the differentiation of a self in one's own family. In J. L. Framo (Ed.), *Family Interaction.* New York: Springer, 1972.

Anthony, E. J., & Koupernik, C. (Eds.) *The Child in His Family: The International Yearbook for Child Psychiatry and Allied Disciplines. Vol 1.* New York: Wiley, 1970.

Bagarozzi, D., & Anderson, S. The evolution of family mythological systems: Considerations for meaning, clinical assessment, and treatment. *Journal of Psychoanalytic Anthropology,* 1982, *5* (1), 71–90.

Bagarozzi, D., & Anderson, S. The use of family myths as an aid to strategic therapy. *Journal of Family Therapy,* 1983, *5,* 145–154.

Bateson, G. *Steps Toward an Ecology of Mind.* New York: Ballantine Books, 1972.

Bateson, G. *Mind and Nature: A Necessary Unity.* New York: E. P. Dutton, 1979.

Bianciardi, M., & Galliano, M. Hypothesizing or provocation: A comparative analysis of two Italian schools of family therapy. *American Journal of Family Therapy,* 1987, *15* (1), 3–18.

Bloch, D. (Ed.) *Techniques of Family Psychotherapy: A Primer.* New York: Grune & Stratton, 1973.

Bloch, D., & LaPerriere, K. Techniques of family therapy: A conceptual frame. In D. Bloch (Ed.), *Techniques of Family Psychotherapy: A Primer.* New York: Grune & Stratton, 1973.

Boszormenyi-Nagy, I. Behavior change through family change. In *Foundations of Contextual Therapy: Collected Papers of Ivan Boszormenyi-Nagy, M.D.* New York: Brunner/Mazel, 1987.

Boszormenyi-Nagy, I., & Spark, M. *Invisible Loyalties: Reciprocity in Intergenerational Family Therapy.* New York: Harper & Row, 1973.

Bowen, M. The use of family therapy in clinical practice. *Comprehensive Psychiatry,* 1966, *7,* 345–374.

Bowen, M. *Family Therapy in Clinical Practice.* New York: Jason Aronson, 1978.

Bowlby, J. *Attachment and Loss. Vol. 1: Attachment.* New York: Basic Books, 1969.

Bowlby, J. *Attachment and Loss. Vol. 2: Separation—Anxiety and Anger.* New York: Basic Books, 1973.

Bowlby, J. *Attachment and Loss. Vol. 3: Loss—Sadness and Depression.* New York: Basic Books, 1980.

Bronowski, J. *The Ascent of Man.* Boston: Little, Brown, 1973.

Bruner, J. S., Jolly, A., & Sylva, K. (Eds.) *Play—Its Role in Development and Evolution.* New York: Basic Books, 1976.

Bruner, J. S., Olver, R.R., & Greenfield, P. *Studies in Cognitive Growth.* New York: WIley, 1966.

Byng-Hall, J. Family myths used as defence in conjoint family therapy. *British Journal of Medical Psychology,* 1973, *46,* 239–250.

Byng-Hall, J. Re-editing family mythology during family therapy. *Journal of Family Therapy,* 1979, *1,* 2–14.

Caprettini, G. P., & Ferraro, G. Mythos/logos. In *Enciclopedia, Vol. 15.* Turin: Einaudi, 1982.

Carter, E. A., & McGoldrick, M. (Eds.) *The Family Life Cycle: A Framework for Family Therapy.* New York: Gardner Press, 1980.

Cigoli, V. (Ed.) *Terapia Familiare: L'Orientamento Psicoanalitico.* Milan: Angeli, 1983.

Coppersmith, E. I. Teaching trainees to think in triads. *Journal of Marital and Family Therapy,* 1983, *11* (1), 61–66.

Cronen, V. E., Johnson, K. M., & Lannaman, J. W. Paradoxes, double binds, and reflexive loops: An alternative theoretical perspective. *Family Process,* 1982, *21* (1), 91–112.

Dare, C., & Pincus, L. Il contratto segreto del matrimonio. In V. Cigoli (Ed.), *Terapia Familiare: L'Orientamente Psicoanalitico.* Milan: Angeli, 1983.

de Nichilo, M. Il sindrome di Atlante: Evoluzione dei miti in terapia familiare. *Crescita,* 1986, *23.*

DiBlasio, P., Fischer, J.-M., & Prata, G. The telephone chart: A cornerstone of the first interview with the family. *Journal of Strategic and Systemic Therapies,* 1986, *5* (1 & 2), 31–44.

Dicks, H. *Marital Tensions. Clinical Studies Toward a Psychological Theory of Interaction.* New York: Basic Books, 1967.

DiNicola, V. F. Family therapy and transcultural psychiatry. Part I: The conceptual basis. *Transcultural Psychiatric Research Review,* 1985a, *22* (2): 81–113.

DiNicola, V. F. Family therapy and transcultural psychiatry. Part II: Portability and culture change. *Transcultural Psychiatric Research Review,* 1985b, *22* (3): 151–180.

DiNicola, V. F. Beyond Babel: Family therapy as cultural translation. *International Journal of Family Psychiatry,* 1986, *7* (2), 179–191.

Donati, P., & Scabini, E. (Eds.) *Le Transformazioni della Famiglia Italiana: Studi Interdisciplinari sulla Famiglia.* Milan: Vita e Pensiero, 1984.

Duhl, F., Kantor, D., & Duhl, B. Learning, space, and action in family therapy: A primer of sculpture. In D. Bloch (Ed.), *Techniques of Family Therapy. A Primer.* New York: Grune & Stratton, 1973.

Efron, D. E. (Ed.) *Journeys: Expansion of the Strategic-Systemic Therapies*. New York: Brunner/Mazel, 1986.

Falicov, C. J. (Ed.) *Cultural Perspectives in Family Therapy*. Rockville, MD: Aspen, 1983.

Falicov, C. J., & Karrer, B. M. Cultural variations in the family life cycle. In E. A. Carter & M. McGoldrick (Eds.), *The Family Life Cycle: A Framework for Family Therapy*. New York: Gardner Press, 1980.

Farrelly, F., & Brandsma, J. *The Beginnings of Provocative Therapy*. Cupertino, CA: META Publications, 1974.

Ferraro, G. *Il Linguaggio del Mito*. Milan: Feltrinelli, 1979.

Ferreira, A. Family myth and homeostasis. *Archives of General Psychiatry*, 1963, *9*, 457–463.

Ferreira, A. Family myths: The covert rules of the relationship. *Confinia Psychiatrica*, 1965, *8*, 15–20.

Ferreira, A. Psychosis and family myth. *American Journal of Psychiatry*, 1967, *21*, 186–197.

Foucault, M. *Power/Knowledge: Selected Interviews and Other Writings 1972–1977* (Edited by C. Gordon). New York: Pantheon, 1980.

Framo, J. L. (Ed.) *Family Interaction: A Dialogue Between Family Researchers and Family Therapists*. New York: Springer, 1972.

Framo, J. L. Family of origin as a therapeutic resource for adults in marital and family therapy: You can and should go home again. *Family Process*, 1976, *15* (2), 193–210.

Framo, J. L. *Explorations in Marital and Family Therapy: Selected Papers of James L. Framo*. New York: Springer, 1982.

Friedman, E. H. Systems and ceremonies: A family view of rites of passage. In E. A. Carter & M. McGoldrick (Eds.), *The Family Life Cycle*. New York: Gardner Press, 1980.

Geertz, C. Blurred genres: The refiguration of social thought. In C. Geertz (Ed.), *Local Knowledge: Further Essays in Interpretive Anthropology*. New York: Basic Books, 1983.

Giacometti, K. Terapia familiare: Un modello di sviluppo e una proposta di classificazione. *Terapia Familiare*, 1979, *6*, 7–32.

Gluckman, M. (Ed.) *Essays on the Ritual of Social Relations*. New York: Humanities Press, 1962a.

Gluckman, M. Les rites de passage. In M. Gluckman (Ed.), *Essays on the Ritual of Social Relations*. New York: Humanities Press, 1962b.

Gurman, A. S. & Kniskern, D. P. (Eds.) *Handbook of Family Therapy*. New York: Brunner/Mazel, 1981.

Haley, J. The family of the schizophrenic: A model system. *Journal of Nervous and Mental Diseases*, 1959, *129*, 337–354.

Haley, J. *Uncommon Therapy: The Psychiatric Techniques of Milton H. Erickson, M.D.* New York: W. W. Norton, 1973.

Haley, J. *Problem-Solving Therapy*. San Francisco: Jossey-Bass, 1976.

Haley, J. Toward a theory of pathological systems. In P. Watzalawick & J. Weakland (Eds.), *The Interactional View*. New York: W. W. Norton, 1977.

Hoffman, L. *Foundations of Family Therapy: A Conceptual Framework for System Change.* New York: Basic Books, 1981.

Hutten, E. H. *La scienza contemporanea: Informazione, spiegazione e significato.* Rome: Armando, 1975.

Imber-Black, E. Odysseys of a learner. In D. Efron (Ed.), *Journeys: Expansion of the Strategic-Systemic Therapies.* New York: Brunner/Mazel, 1986.

Izard, M., & Smith, P. (Eds.) *La Fonction Symbolique.* Paris: Gallimard, 1979.

James, W. *The Principles of Psychology* (Vol. 53 in *Great Books of the Western World*). Chicago: William Benton, 1952. First published in New York: Henry Holt, 1890.

Keith, D., & Whitaker, C. Play therapy: A paradigm for work with families. *Journal of Marital and Family Therapy,* 1981, 7 (3), 243–254.

Koestler, A. Association and bisociation. In J. S. Bruner, A. Jolly, & K. Sylva (Eds.), *Play—Its Role in Development and Evolution.* New York: Basic Books, 1976.

Koestler, A. *Janus: A Summing Up.* New York: Random House, 1978.

Leach, E. Ritual. In *International Encyclopedia of the Social Sciences, Vol. 23.* New York: Macmillan, 1968.

Lemaire, J. G. La réalité informe, le mythe structure. *Dialogue,* 1984, 2.

Lévi-Strauss, C. *The Naked Man* (Trans. by J. Weightman and D. Weightman). Vol. 4 in *Introduction to a Science of Mythology Series.* New York: Harper & Row, 1981.

Liotti, G. Attaccamento, sé e famiglia: Tre sistemi interconnessi. *Terapia Familiare,* 1983, *13,* 21–30.

Madanes, C. *Strategic Family Therapy.* San Francisco: Jossey-Bass, 1981.

McGoldrick, M., Pearce, J. K., & Giordano, J. *Ethnicity and Family Therapy.* New York: Guilford Press, 1982.

Minuchin, S. The use of an ecological framework in the treatment of a child. In E. J. Anthony & C. Koupernik (Eds.), *The Child in His Family.* New York: Wiley, 1970.

Minuchin, S. *Families and Family Therapy.* Cambridge, MA: Harvard University Press, 1974.

Minuchin, S., & Fishman, H. C. *Family Therapy Techniques.* Cambridge, MA: Harvard University Pres, 1981.

Montalvo, B., & Haley, J. In defense of child therapy. *Family Process,* 1973, *12,* 227–244.

Napier, A. Y., & Whitaker, C. A. *The Family Crucible.* New York: Harper & Row, 1978.

Neill, J. R., & Kniskern, D. P. (Eds.) *From Psyche to System: The Evolving Therapy of Carl Whitaker.* New York: Guilford Press, 1982.

Neisser, U. *Cognitive Psychology.* Englewood Cliffs, NJ: Prentice-Hall, 1967.

Nicolò-Corigliano, A. M. Le relazione di coppia in gravidenza. *Crescita,* 1985, *12.*

Paolino, T. J., & McCrady, B. S. (Eds.) *Marriage and Marital Therapy: Psychoanalytic, Behavioral and Systems Theory Perspectives.* New York: Brunner/Mazel, 1978.

Papp, P., Silverstein, O., & Carter, E. A. Family sculpting in preventive work with "well families." *Family Process*, 1973, *12*, 197–212.

Piperno, R. La funzione della provocazione nel mantenimento omeostatico dei sistemi rigidi. *Terapia Familiare*, 1979, *5*, 39–50.

Pontalti, C. Mythos e Logos nella mitologia familiare: Riflessioni dell'esperienza clinica. *Archivio Psicologia, Neurologia e Psichiatria*, 1980, *2*, 178–183.

Propp, V. *Morphology of the Folktale* (2nd Edition). (Edited by L. A. Wagner, translated from Russian by L. Scott). Houston: University of Texas Press, 1968.

Ricci, C., & Selvini Palazzoli, M. Interaction complexity and communication. *Family Process*, 1984, *23* (2), 169–176.

Rosman, B., Minuchin, S., & Liebman, R. Family lunch session: An introduction to family therapy in anorexia nervosa. *American Journal of Orthopsychiatry*, 1975, *45* (5), 846–853.

Rotondo, G. La modifica della struttura cognitiva della famiglia nel processo terapeutico. *Terapia Familiare*, 1983, *13*, 47–70.

Saccu, C. Il bambino da oggetto di cura a strumento di formazione relazionale. In M. Andolfi & D. Piccone (Eds.), *La Formazione Relazionale. Individuo e Gruppo nel Processo di Apprendimento*. Rome: Institute of Family Therapy, 1985.

Sager, C. *Marriage Contracts and Couples Therapy*. New York: Brunner/Mazel, 1976.

Satir, V. *Conjoint Family Therapy: A Guide to Theory and Technique*. Palo Alto: Science and Behavior Books, 1967.

Satir, V. *Peoplemaking*. Palo Alto: Science and Behavior Books, 1972.

Scabini, E. Evoluzione dei legami intergenerazionali e tipi di funzionamento familiare. In P. Donati & E. Scabini (Eds.), *Le Trasformazioni della Famiglia Italiana: Studi Interdisciplinari sulla Famiglia*. Milan: Vita e Pensiero, 1984.

Scabini, E. *L'organizzazione famiglia tra crisi e sviluppo*. Milan: Angeli, 1985.

Scheflen, A. E. *Body Language and the Social Order*. Englewood Cliffs, NJ: Prentice-Hall, 1972.

Seltzer, W. J., & Seltzer, M. R. Material, myth and magic: A cultural approach to family therapy. *Family Process*, 1983, *22* (1), 3–14.

Selvini Palazzoli, M. Why a long interval between sessions? The therapeutic control of the family-therapist suprasystem. In M. Andolfi & I. Zwerling (Eds.), *Dimensions of Family Therapy*. New York: Guilford Press, 1980.

Selvini Palazzoli, M., Boscolo, L., Cecchin, G., & Prata, G. The treatment of children through the brief treatment of their parents. *Family Process*, 1974, *13*, 429–442.

Selvini Palazzoli, M., Boscolo, L., Cecchin, G., & Prata, G. *Paradox and Counterparadox: A New Model in the Therapy of the Family in Schizophrenic Transaction*. New York: Jason Aronson, 1978a.

Selvini Palazzoli, M., Boscolo, L., Cecchin, G., & Prata, G. Ritualized prescriptions in family therapy: Odd days and even days. *Journal of Marriage and Family Counseling*, 1978b, *4*, 3–9.

Selvini Palazzoli, M., Boscolo, L., Cecchin, G., & Prata, G. Hypothesizing-circularity-neutrality: Three guidelines for the conductor of the session. *Family Process*, 1980a, 19 (1), 3–12.

Selvini Palazzoli, M., Boscolo, L., Cecchin, G., & Prata, G. The problem of the referring person. *Journal of Marital and Family Therapy*, 1980b, 6, 3–9.

Selvini Palazzoli, M., & Prata, G. Snares in family therapy. *Journal of Marital and Family Therapy*, 1982, 8 (4), 443–450.

Simon, F. B., Stierlin, H., & Wynne, L. C. *The Language of Family Therapy: A Systemic Vocabulary and Sourcebook*. New York: Family Process Press, 1985.

Sluzki, C. The coevolutionary process in initiating family therapy. *Family Process*, 1975, 12, 67–78.

Sluzki, C. Marital therapy from a systems perspective. In T. J. Paolino & B. S. McCrady (Eds.), *Marriage and Marital Therapy: Psychoanalytic, Behavioral and Systems Theory Perspectives*. New York: Brunner/Mazel, 1978.

Sluzki, C. E., & Ransom, D. C. (Eds.) *Double Bind: The Foundation of the Communicational Approach to the Family*. New York: Grune & Stratton, 1976.

Smith, P. Aspects de l'organisation des rites. In M. Izard & P. Smith (Eds.), *La Fonction Symbolique*. Paris: Gallimard, 1979.

Soccorsi, S., & Palma, G. Dalla crisi al rapporto in crisi. *Terapia Familiare*, 1982, 12, 5–18.

Stanton, M. D. Fusion, compression, diversion and the workings of paradox: A theory of therapeutic/systemic change. *Family Process*, 1984, 23 (2), 135–168.

Stierlin, H. *Delegation und Familie*. Frankfurt: Suhrkamp, 1978.

Turner, V. W. *The Ritual Process. Structure and Anti-Structure*. Chicago: Aldine, 1969.

Ugazio, V. Ipotezzazione e processo terapeutico. *Terapia Familiare*, 1984, 16, 27–54.

Valeri, V. Gioco. In *Enciclopedia, Vol. 6*. Turin: Einaudi, 1979.

Valeri, V. Rito. In *Enciclopedia, Vol. 12*. Turin: Einaudi, 1981.

Walsh, F. (Ed.) *Normal Family Processes*. New York: Guilford Press, 1982.

Watzlawick, P., & Weakland, J. (Eds.) *The Interactional View: Studies at the Mental Research Institute, 1965–1974*. New York: W. W. Norton, 1977.

Watzlawick, P., Weakland, J., & Fisch, R. *Change*. New York: W. W. Norton, 1974.

Weakland, J. The double bind hypothesis of schizophrenia and three party interaction. In C. E. Sluzki & D. C. Ransom (Eds.), *Double Bind: The Foundation of the Communicational Approach to the Family*. New York: Grune & Stratton, 1976.

Weeks, G. R., & L'Abate, L. *Paradoxical Psychotherapy: Theory and Practice with Individuals, Couples, and Families*. New York: Brunner/Mazel, 1982.

Whitaker, C. A. Psychotherapy of the absurd with special emphasis on the psychotherapy of aggression. *Family Process*, 1975, 14, 1–16.

Whitaker, C. A. From psyche to system. In J. R. Neill & D. P. Kniskern (Eds.), *From Psyche to System: The Evolving Therapy of Carl Whitaker*. New York: Guilford Press, 1982.

Whitaker, C. A. *Il Gioco e L'Assurdo.* (Translated and edited by G. Vella and W. Trasarti Sponti). Rome: Astrolabio, 1984.

Whitaker, C. A., & Keith, D. V. Symbolic-experiential family therapy. In A. S. Gurman & D. P. Kniskern (Eds.), *Handbook of Family Therapy.* New York: Brunner/Mazel, 1981.

Williamson, D. S. Personal authority via termination of the intergenerational hierarchical boundary: A "new" stage in the family life cycle. *Journal of Marital and Family Therapy,* 1981, 7 (4), 441–452.

Winnicott, D. W. *Playing and Reality.* New York: Basic Books, 1971.

Wolin, S. J., & Bennett, L. A. Family rituals. *Family Process,* 1984, 23, 401–420.

Wynne, I. C. The epigenesis of relational systems: A model for understanding family development. *Family Process,* 1984, 23 (3), 297–318.

Zuk, G. H. The side-taking function in family therapy. *American Journal of Orthopsychiatry,* 1968, 38 (3), 553–559.

Index of Family Cases

IP: Marina, 10-year-old daughter
Training Group, IFT, Rome
Supervised in Italian by Dr. Andolfi

2. *Therapy* (pp. 69–70)
Gabrieli Family
IP: Laura, 7-year-old daughter
Conducted in Italian by Dr. Marco
  Bianciardi
Supervised by Dr. Andolfi

3. *Consultation* (pp. 72–73)
Johnson Family
IPs: Julius and Dylan, 7 and 9
Hahnemann Medical College,
  Philadelphia, USA, 1980
Consultation in English by Dr.
  Andolfi

4. *Marital Therapy* (pp. 73–74, 229,
231)
Pantella Couple
Dr. Andolfi's private studio, Rome
Cotherapy conducted in Italian by
  Drs. Andolfi and Marcella de
  Nichilo

5. *Therapy* (pp. 75–77)
Garofalo Family
IP: Giorgia, 16-year-old daughter
Training Group, IFT, Rome
Conducted in Italian by Dr. Andolfi

6. *Therapy* (pp. 79–81)
Neri Family
School of Family Therapy, IFT,
  Rome
Conducted in Italian by a student
  therapist
Supervised by Dr. Andolfi

7. *Consultation* (p. 83)
Schultz Family
IP: Enuretic boy
Workshop in Hartford,
  Connecticut, USA, 1983
Consultation in English by Dr.
  Andolfi

8. *Consultation* (pp. 83–85)
Hiller Family
IP: John, 20-year-old son

Hahnemann Medical College,
  Philadelphia, USA, 1978
Consultation in English by Dr.
  Andolfi

9. *Marital Therapy* (p. 86)
Steiner Couple
Seminar, Esalen Institute,
  California, USA, 1984
Consultation in English by Dr.
  Andolfi

CHAPTER 5

1. *Film Vignette* (pp. 94–96, 230, 231)
"Fanny and Alexander" by Ingmar
  Bergman

2. *Therapy* (pp. 100–110)
Vianini Family from Rome
IP: Marco, 13-year-old son
Dr. Andolfi's private studio, Rome
Conducted in Italian by Dr. Andolfi

CHAPTER 6

1. *Therapy* (pp. 117–118)
Working with the "Family lunch
  session" with anorectic families
School, IFT, Rome
Conducted in Italian by Dr. Pina
  Longoni
Supervised by Dr. Andolfi

2. *Therapy* (pp. 118–123)
"A Doormat"

3. *Therapy* (pp. 120–123)
Venturi Family/Couple
IP: 49-year-old husband
IFT, Rome
Conducted in Italian by Drs.
  Carmine Saccu and Paolo Menghi
Supervised by Dr. Andolfi

4. *Therapy* (pp. 124–131)
Grillo Family from Rome
School of Family Therapy, IFT,
  Rome
Conducted in Italian by Dr. Rita
  Ferri
Supervised by Dr. Andolfi

Author Index

231

Subject Index

233